Handwritten inscription:

Dear B[...]
M[...]
Thoughts" yield a
golden harvest.
Love, John

The Fruit of
Your Thoughts

Insights of Peter Rosen

The Fruit of Your Thoughts

Insights of Peter Rosen

by John Roberts

Roaring Lion Publishing Company

The Fruit of Your Thoughts
can be purchased in retail stores
or by mail from:

Roaring Lion Publishing Company
P. O. Box 471
Boise, Idaho
83701

Visa or Mastercard orders call
1-800-358-1929

Please add $4.00 shipping and handling for all orders.
Idaho residents add $1.00 sales tax.

Written by John Roberts
Edited by Josephine Jones
Cover Designed by Neil Marwehe
Cover Photo by Andy Burnett
Text Layout by Jeffrey Conger

First Edition - 1997

ISBN 0-878682-02-4 : $20.00

Library of Congress Card Number
96-93130

Table of Contents

To
My mother, Yula Roberts Turner,
for whom I hold a special place of love.

Acknowledgments

I would like to express my gratitude to Janice Wittenborn for introducing me to Peter in October of 1991, Gay Whitesides for reading and editing every first draft with enthusiastic praise, Carol Lyons and Paula Jones for copy editing and advice, Suzanne Lewis for encouragement, Chris Binion for cutting away the extraneous to smooth the prose, Nancy Budge for reading drafts simultaneously from the views of corporate skeptic and open-minded believer, and Josephine Jones for editing and compiling.

"The golden-headed stalk of wheat that ripens in the warmth of the sun bows its head from the sheer weight of its treasure. The immature stalk arrogantly stands when it ought to bow to the one, God's sun blazing in the sky. It rattles its empty head, which so far is devoid of the golden kernels of life.

The weeds, the imitators, also come and sow their bitter fruit. But behold the day of harvest is upon you and the reapers are in your midst. The golden lord of the harvest did not die like a dry and withered seed, nor was he buried in the barren soil. No! He has risen from the grave as a life-giving spirit, the light of lights and king of kings.

And how could he mistake the seeds his own hand had planted in our hearts? Yes, yes, yes, we are his golden field of wheat! And the kernels of his luminous life."

—Peter Rosen

Foreword

Intended as a practical guide to living fully and abundantly, this book is a work of love inspired by seminars given by Peter Rosen of Mystic Mountain. I have chosen to follow Peter as my practical, spiritual teacher, and gathered the following information by taking careful notes at Peter's seminars over the last five years. To limit omissions or misunderstandings, Peter graciously reviewed this book and carefully amended misinterpretations. The words and ideas are primarily his, the arrangement mine. I occasionally include my own insights. An asterisk (*) indicates a direct quotation of Peter Rosen. Read this book slowly, perhaps even out loud, and you are likely to feel Peter's loving energy.

—John Roberts, 1996

"And the word of God became man, that you may also learn from a man how a man becomes a god."

—Clement of Alexandria

Chapter 1

Awareness

"If you control your thoughts, you control your destiny."
—Peter Rosen

Stairway to Heaven

The first rung of your stairway to heaven is on earth. To succeed at spiritual development, you must first handle your material stuff. Attaining prosperity, health and friendship brings out the virtues, talents and tools you need to reach greater heights.

As you climb the mountain to heaven, others help you along the way, but only you can do the climbing. To complete the task, you must drop your unnecessary baggage. The experience is so rarefied that unless you maintain laser-like focus, you can lose your way.

Have high ideals and beautiful visions. The easy way is to put one foot in front of the other. Most people think this way is hard, but it is easy. Just start climbing. Every step gets you closer to the top. Take it a step at a time with finances, health and relationships. Master these and you will have enough self-esteem to succeed spiritually.

Master the ABCs

You deserve to live pleasantly and happily. You have the choice and the power to make life anything you want. You are a child of a very opulent form of energy, and can have physical, mental and divine truth. However, it is insane to work beyond your own level.

You must master the ABCs first. Take a moment to write down your answers to the following:

A....Get the physical body working

What areas do I need to give attention to and correct?
What maintenance program will I start?
What will I start today?

B....Think logically and rationally

Do I have unfocused thoughts?
Will I examine the conclusions I have drawn?
Do any of my thoughts create emotional distress?
What thoughts will I change? How?
Do I seek and love truth in all areas of my life?

C....Get my spiritual self functioning

How can I tune in to my inner knowingness?
What helps me focus on my purpose?
How can I be passionate about my usefulness?

These are the ABCs. As you see the fruit of your thoughts, you realize their limitless power.

Responsibility Generates Power

We are all saved from having true power until we have mastered the ABCs and can use this power responsibly. The derelict on the street is saved by the weakness of his thoughts. Deluded with negativity, his sluggish thoughts manifest slowly. This saves him from harm. If we had a wish-fulfilling tree before we knew responsibility, we would destroy ourselves.

Listen to your words. You can't be given power until you're responsible. Eliminate phrases and thoughts like these: "I'm so broke." "I could kill him." "I hate." "I feel like death." "I'm so old."

The more responsible we become with our thoughts, the more powerful we become. As we function with integrity, we begin to produce the results of our thoughts quickly.

The ABCs work best when not taken too seriously. The ego embraces seriousness. Think of them and other ideas discussed here as practical, healthy and wise blueprints.

The ABCs are ways to have light in your heart or to be light-hearted. When we are light-hearted, we are sincere, flexible and conscientious.

Take the Enriching, Discard the Rest

We are authentic when we take responsibility for ourselves. Uncomfortable people often seek the spiritual to avoid confronting what is wrong in their daily life. They want someone else to take care of them. Choose what enriches you, and do not rely on others to take care of you.

The contrast to an enriching life is the hell we create when we do not accept responsibility for creating what we want. Much of life is spent gaining awareness and learning how to manifest what we desire. Happiness is our natural state. Learn to choose it, even when those around you are unhappy.

Life is too beautiful to run away from. Life is yours to live in all its glory. You can burn as brightly as the sun rising on the side of a mountain. You really cannot fail. Just don't look back. It's a new sunrise. Step by step is how it's done. Discard the old day and embrace the new dawn. A luminous light guides you.

You can never go back, no matter how beautiful it was. You can never step into the same river twice. It's always moving. To be enriched, you can look down the mountain to see how high you've climbed. You'll find the peak is closer than you thought.

Truthful Decisions Simplify Life

When making decisions, your great inner tutor, intuition, speaks the nonjudgmental truth of your heart. True answers come when you stop the chatter and listen to the knowingness of your heart. Do not confuse your emotions with your heart! Your emotions can sway you away from the truth.

When we get out of our heads and into our hearts, everything starts to come true. On the purest level, the heart always speaks truth. Discern what is true and what is not. Do not make decisions based on feelings, analyses or beliefs. Make decisions by truthfully and simply assessing your experiences. What resulted from your past choices?

It's Perfectly All Right to Be You

You are free when you see yourself alone (all one). You see life as perfect when you truthfully see it as it is now. Every step you take becomes more, not less. You create what you put effort into. There is only self-imposed limitation.

It's wonderful to know what you want and like. Make those things concrete and write them down. Would you like to work less, more or differently? Your life is better when you have valuable objectives. When you fill your reality with aliveness and peace, these become of highest value because they allow your enlightenment.

Words can be lies, but actions reveal the truth. Your actions and their resulting circumstances tell others what you believe to be true. You fail only when you try to be something other than yourself. When you act or talk only to please others, you must defend those behaviors. The secret to inner peace is to be yourself.

You need to be authentic and to be around genuine people. Anything other than authenticity is unacceptable. Authenticity gives peace and banishes fear and anxiety. When you are consistently authentic, your radiance shows that you embrace the light. Your body, health and looks change.

Your affirmation becomes, "I want a perfect body, health, prosperity and peace. It is possible to live as long as I wish." Physical health represents how we feel about ourselves. When you stand tall, you feel up.

When we are authentic, we no longer feel guilt, and our words and thoughts allow us to enjoy life and to not suffer. When we experience truth, we live without effort. Life is play.

The Divine Always Lets Us Decide Again

We are all Children of the King. The universe approves a requisition that says, "Ask for what you want, and I will see that it happens." When we say, "I'm not supposed to want," the universe answers, "Fine, you will get nothing. You have one more wish."

Write down clearly what you want and set your mind toward it. Truth comes in work clothes. Success calls for putting a little "umph" in the try, and sooner than you expect, you will "triumph." Worship triumph in all things and you live without apology.

To know what you want and not do it is to deprive yourself. Whatever affirms life for you is your spiritual truth. Examine the foundation of your tenets of faith, then free yourself from the useless bondage and shackles of self-defeating beliefs. Reach high. The sweetest fruit ripens at the end of the limb where the sun shines the brightest and it takes great courage to reach it.

The Center Is Right Here, Right Now

To get an accurate reading on your life, see it from the perspective of now. To determine your accurate weight, you must first balance the scales by setting them at the zero or center point.

The center point of how you are doing is also determined by a proper calibration. You cannot look at it from the past or the future. The center is right here, right now. You can be nowhere else. You will be filled with joy if you let go of the "shoulds" and "musts."

The centered person is at peace and alert, responding minute by minute to the here and now. An enlightened Being enjoys the freedom of not living in the dead past or imagined future. The centered person enjoys what is, wherever he is, without demands or addictions. Finding your center is to "be here now."

The Truth Sets Us Free

Are you ready for an element of surprise in your life? Do not think that you know it all and have all knowledge from past teachings. That would be a scary and corrupt thought, like a fool dreaming he's awake while still sleeping.

Jesus taught the principle that truth will set you free. The truth is, you are enlightened pretending not to be.

Enlightenment leads to freedom. Freedom is not getting addicted to the "stuff" of the bodies. The real treasure is beyond "stuff." If you want to be free, get out of your head and into your heart, your center of knowingness. Drink from the cup of truth, an invisible elixir that you feel in your heart.

The Eye of the Needle

Jesus taught in one of the parables that it would be easier for a camel to go through the eye of a needle than for a rich man to enter the Kingdom of Heaven. "Rich" means the person who is always hungry for more and never satisfied. No matter how much wealth the rich man accumulates, he feels impoverished. He demands more and more, and can't enjoy what he has.

The rich person's astral body is swollen with desire for more. He cannot get into the kingdom of heaven or be content now, because he cannot find the center point in life. He cannot get through the center of the eye of the needle.

The camel is content living in the desert under the hot sun, trusting that an oasis will come and that it can find nourishment where there appears to be none. Due to its contentment, the camel's astral form is small and can fit through the eye of the needle. But if the camel becomes gluttonous its stomach expands. Then it cannot fit through the needle's eye, the vertical slit in the brick wall of a desert town, that it could ease through when empty.

If you enjoy what you have, you can be content now. Only the person who is content with what he has can be prosperous. The person who has compulsions of "I need . . . I must have more . . . Give me, give me, give me" will always be poor. He will never experience enough.

Pricked by the Thorn of Discernment

When your ego is huge, it is ready to be pricked by the thorn of discernment. The huge ego keeps saying, "I need." No, you do not need. Burst that huge balloon. There is a heaven world and a hell world. The hell reality states, "I need, I have to" and is full of addictions. The heaven realm says, "I want to." Live in the heaven realm of "I want to," rather than the hell realm of "I have to" or "I should."

What You Want Wants You

Thoughts create your expectations, which create your reality. What you expect you get. If you focus on what you don't want, you will get more of it. Fortunately, life always gives you a chance to change your mind.

If you experience anger, start focusing on how good it feels to be peaceful. If you are a smoker, visualize yourself feeling good as a nonsmoker. Focus on what you want to become.

Just a Simple Needle and Thread

The old Sage sat making wonderful garments. He never got flustered or fell into despair, because he knew there were no problems, only decisions to make. He knew that just a little patience makes all things possible.

One day the King gave the old Sage a pair of gold and diamond inlaid scissors. The old Sage asked the King what he should do with scissors. He told the King that scissors cut apart, but what he did was put things together. All he needed was a simple needle and thread.

The Sage wasn't talking about clothing of a physical nature, but of a divine nature. All he needed was the one-pointed golden needle of focus to repair the fabric of life.

Everyone has a spiritual force-field of wealth, but it must be tapped through focus. We are powerful, and wherever we focus, there we reap our dividends.

Know What You Want

It takes a very special type of awareness and focus to know what you want. Tape-record your every word for 24 hours and note your thoughts. At the end of that 24-hour period, review what you held in your mind. That is what you manifest in the present, as well as what you create cumulatively in the future.

You can also discover what thoughts you have held in your mind simply by looking at the circumstances of your life. This is no great secret, but it is so obvious that it eludes many of you. You manifest your reality in direct proportion to your thoughts, which either enhance or impoverish you.

Choose Heaven Today

When you choose heaven today, you start appreciating and living in a wonderful and miraculous world of blessings. You begin to see the roses, not the thorns. You see only what you want and know that it wants you. This is the Kingdom of God on earth.

You choose heaven today by looking for the points of beauty along the road. When some difficulty occurs, just turn it around and see it from a different angle. Don't choose to think that people purposefully cut in front of you in traffic to offend you. Personalizing issues makes them difficult emotionally.

We Live in a World of Cause and Effect

Your thoughts weave the fabric of your life. Your thoughts are the causes and your environment their effect. When you focus on disaster you invite disaster, because the universe gives you what you think. You are only as safe as your thoughts. Your thoughts create your reality. They are your safety or your peril. This does not mean you cannot have a broad perspective on life, nor consider all kinds of issues. You can be discerning without dwelling on what you wouldn't want to bring into your reality. Plan practical steps, free of anxiety.

In a world of cause and effect you cannot fail unless you have failure thoughts. The universe provides us with all that we want. Though the spiritual realm is beyond thought, spiritual energy empowers us to think. Control the fabric of your thoughts and weave a new life that is vibrantly yours. If your heart is in it, you will have the passion and energy to create what you desire.

Your Word is Your Wand

The practical miracle is that your word is your wand. Miracles occur every moment, and you hold their power in your hands. You do not need a guru or someone to do it for you. You have the ability to live miracles all the time. When you forget this, you seek approval from outside yourself.

For too long, some of us have allowed others into our heads. Others can affect us positively or negatively. Watch who you choose to be open to. Be aware of who influences you and how.

As you grow in awareness of your creative power, you will notice that your thoughts manifest results more and more quickly. To manifest your reality consciously, combine focused thoughts with passionate energy.

Slowing your thoughts gives you a greater ability to visualize. Once you gain control of your thought processes, you see what you want. Use your creative abilities. As you do, you will know and visualize more.

Seeing Through Illusion

What we habitually express unconsciously becomes a statement of fact, an affirmation that affects our life. Continued long enough, our nervous system accepts it, and we become confused.

The Sanskrit word "maya" means "illusion." Don't despair, because you would just be despairing over an illusion. Things are not as they appear to be and that's why they're illusory. Everyone sees things through his own eyes, but there is one reality independent of opinion. The answer to the illusion is to focus your thoughts in the here and now. Time is always now.

We can be so mentally distracted that it projects us elsewhere. We can't be here now when we daydream or are distracted and unaware of our addicted thought journeys. Do not turn your mind loose without direction.

Random thoughts can make us drunk and cause us to bump into walls. We get caught in the illusion of life. Physical glands release chemicals that create drugged and confused thoughts that keep us from perceiving what life really is all about. Be very focused on what you do and think. Understand why you think certain things.

Confusion breeds death because it pulls you down. You can choose between life and death. Consciousness is the cure. Proclaim this affirmation: "I live my life with the highest values and as much honesty and integrity as I can grasp."

How do you become conscious? Monitor and then choose what you think. Exercise your consciousness by doing one thing at a time. See one thought at a time. Clarity leads to unlimited power.

To pierce the veil of maya:

- Hold only razor-sharp objective thoughts.
- Have one thought at a time.
- Be acutely aware.
- See each thought as a picture.
- Be organized.
- Keep it simple.
- Love truth.

When you have an emotion, examine your conclusions that led to the emotion. Were they correct?

Love Is the Catalyst

The love you share is the catalyst for your transformation. Your contagious love and empathy will rub off on others. Let the love catalyst begin with you. Be decent, polite and genuine because that is who you are — a decent, polite and genuine person.

Be Solution-Minded

There are two types of people in the world:

- Those who see problems.
- Those who see solutions.

Whom would you bet on?

Nothing happens for those who see only problems.

They can't even agree with each other. The only way to succeed is to be solution-minded. This enables you to powerfully transform your world.

You are never checkmated or have no way out of your problems. There are always solutions in the universe, no matter how checkmated you feel. The solution to a problem involves making a decision. Know what you want and start in that direction.

No one can stop you from doing or being anything you want. You are a free moral agent with incredible power. "Yes, I can do it . . . If it is to be, it is up to me. . . . If I have challenges, I can always find solutions" is the self-talk that gets you through. To accomplish the best of your desires, focus on solutions.

Be a Living Solution

If we desire in our hearts to be loving, peaceful and happy, we are living solutions in our world. Solution-minded friends create a bond of unity and produce harmonious results in their environments. Through these solution-minded friendships we become a family blessed with abundance.

See lovable qualities in others. Quit trying to make others over. Don't be a fixer. Don't seek approval from others. No one excels when he tries to prove his worthiness to another.

What is your heart's desire? If it is for flowers, you will beget beauty. If it is for thorns, you will beget hardship. One's authentic desire can become peace. Do not focus on conflict. Focus on how you can have peace. Heaven is right before you now. Learn to manifest it with your thoughts.

Out of the heart's abundance, the mouth speaks. What you speak reflects your heart. As the heart becomes pure, your world becomes pure. As you become solution-minded, your blue-green planet shines like a jewel.

Dark Thoughts Are Thieves

Thieves break in and steal on the level of the intellect. The thieves are your dark thoughts. Thoreau wrote, "The mass of men lead lives of quiet desperation" (*Walden*). Set sail free of desperation. What in the world is there to be desperate about? When the worst that could happen is that you could die, and you realize you've done that before, you live with less fear.

Watch diligently that your heart does not become infested with the worms of worry and doubt. These create heartache. Avoid what makes you sick at heart. Negative thoughts are not valuable. Concentrate on what no one can steal. Hold your energy, focus and time deep within your heart. The riches of the Kingdom are inside.

If It's Not Working, Do the Opposite

If you argue and fight at home, you will create discord anywhere. To avoid fighting, just do the opposite of what you do to start fights. You reap what you sow. If it's not working, do the opposite.

When artists can't see what is missing in a painting, they hold the painting up to the mirror to see it in reverse. When you can't see what is wrong in life, hold it up to a mirror. Look at things backwards for a new perspective. See the solution, not the problem. Write down five great ways to totally destroy a relationship and then do the opposite. To not do the negatives, be attentive. Do their opposites. How would this affect your current relationships?

With employment, write down ten great ways to get fired and then do the opposite every day. Stop doing what doesn't work. Do not over-analyze or you will get "paralysis by analysis."

Knowing when to cut your losses demonstrates wisdom and courage. Examine your visualizations, remembering that what you think is what you expect, and what you expect is what you get. God makes sure universal laws are consistent. Cause and effect will continue to operate, so it's insane to expect different results from the same cause.

Love yourself and others. Treat others the way you want to be treated. Your attitude creates your expectations. To the degree that your attitude is positive or negative, your life is positive or negative. When your thoughts change, so will your disposition.

Don't Try to Find Something Wrong

Practice getting up in the morning and reviewing all the wonderful things you can experience that day. Laugh at the challenges and chuckle at yourself. The Universe will open its doors to you.

Never focus on your limitations. Acknowledge your strengths. Be around those who love you and encourage you. Do the same for others, and life will become miraculous.

King David said, "Whoever wants to enjoy life, and wishes to see good times, must keep from speaking evil and stop telling lies. He must turn away from evil and do good; he must strive for peace in his heart" (Psalms 34:13-14 quoted in I Peter 3:10-11). When everything is going great on the inside, the outside world reflects it. Never say anything about yourself that you do not wish to be true. Do not think things or say things to others that you don't want to manifest.

Life can be rich with peace, happiness, serenity and material prosperity. Why do you have to justify yourself? You owe no one an apology for being on this plane of reality. You do what you do. You are here to learn to live more harmoniously with the universe. Say what you want, and it will be yours.

Personalities Reflect Thoughts

You see everyone through your various personality characteristics. To see clearly, work toward being whole and balanced within yourself. A whole person is authentic and internally honest. A whole person knows that what he sees is what he gets. Your flaws die from lack of attention.

Be in the driver's seat. Focus on where you're going and release attachment to your imperfections. If you don't know where you're going, you just sit or end up somewhere else. When your heart says "Yes," go for it! You can often do things you don't think you can. Your drive is the talent within you.

Your success depends on how you use your energy. Creative people learn from the past, but focus on decisions that lead to healthy use of energy. Unhealthy use of energy leads to abuse of your abilities and is so chaotic that you become frantic. Balance and direct the energy that drives your visions.

It Takes Courage to Grow

You are free to grow. You travel independently and alone. You cannot be responsible for bringing anyone with you. Others have to choose for their own self-realization. Embark on this journey with courage and you'll find God. You're home at last.

You live fenced in by your beliefs, and fear to step beyond their boundaries. It is possible to go beyond them, but not easy. This journey takes much courage. You are perfectible. The way is straight up the mountain. You'll fall and hurt yourself many times, but despite the bruises, never give up. Seek life by living it. Don't let your quest distract you from the now. Abandon even the quest and you are free forever.

What Is Right for You?

Many will be angry at you when you act in freedom. Fences of belief are only lies told so often they imprison the mind. Do what you want to. Go where you want to go. Be who you want to be. You are totally free to think on your own.

Be conscious of doing things differently and not always in a routine way. Make sure your morning meditations vary. When you go to bed at night, change sides of the bed and get up on the other side. Shift things around. Go to work a different way.

Being conscious expands your perceptions. The doorway to higher consciousness involves becoming conscious first. Preconceived ideas often block perception. Watch and listen to what is around you. See how you feel. Perceptions differ because of struggles. Each person has his own mountains to climb.

Being aware and fully conscious of that around us can teach us. Ecstasy and bliss are the fringe benefits of attaining your highest value, your peak.

Chapter 2

Balance

"Live with confidence
no matter how many times you trip or fall."
—Peter Rosen

Get Your Balance

It doesn't take long for a lifetime to pass. It passes as quickly as a good weekend. When everything goes too fast, go slower. When things go too slowly, go faster. Get your balance. That is how you find your center point in life.

Watch your thoughts when they start going too fast. Do one thing at a time, in order and perfectly. Never hurry. You'll come to see the difference this makes. You can be urgent at times, but do not respond in a panic. Leave on time so you do not have to rush. When you rush, you beat up on yourself and people feel it.

Slow it down. You are a heroic, courageous being who becomes stronger with each challenge you overcome. You have the strength for your upcoming challenges when you seek the truth. Live the examined life. Your heart will say "yes" one day at a time.

Why not be peaceful now, rather than during the next lifetime or at age 84? See the futility of so many distresses now, before you get old and near this lifetime's death. Know what is valuable. You don't take the stuff of this life with you. Self-worth leads to acts and expressions that continue forever.

Honor Your Own Value

When you relax and allow yourself to be, wonderful things happen. In the craziness of life you feel tense, rushed, pressured. This form of self-sabotage results from low self-esteem.

Self-esteem means to value and honor yourself. See value in your own being and hold yourself in highest esteem. What you consider precious, you protect. Increase your self-esteem. Value your own Beingness and show appreciation for it.

Self-esteem thrives on excellence. You see the smudges and clean the windows. You pick up the trash because you know something changes inside of you when you perform with excellence.

Give What You Value the Best of Care

Your value is far more than any monetary measurement. When you don't value yourself, you harm yourself. When you see the value of your own worth as precious and wonderful, you give yourself the finest food, plenty of exercise, good thoughts, prosperity and all good things. Love yourself. Jesus said, "Love thy neighbor as thyself" (Matthew 19:19). You cannot love your neighbor more than you are able to love yourself.

The greatest challenge is to just do it. You are worth the effort. What is it that you imagine for yourself? Do what you must do, despite public opinion. This calls for personal integrity. It starts with the little issues such as sweeping the corners. For your aura to be whole, do not neglect those little things. The difference between the extraordinary and the ordinary person is in the little extras that someone will do for nothing.

The value of your work is who you become by doing it. Forget about what is behind you. You can never step back. The past is gone. Stop holding on or you will just get older each moment of the day. The grace of God often prevents you from knowing all your past in this life and past lives.

What you have behind and before you is your sum total now. Go back one year or ten years; you were less, not more. The value of your experiences creates who you are now. Some people are pretty great just because they survived their families. Stay present and bask in the moment. Here and now you think and act to create your future.

You Can Bless the World

Your acts of worship are reflected in how you dress, drive, walk, work and interact with others. Working with integrity and high self-esteem and performing with excellence are holy acts. God is the most excellent vision.

Only you can make the world a blessing. No one is coming to the rescue. You bring light out of darkness. Dedicate and consecrate yourself to the light, bright and luminous. If you worship love, you are love.

Know what you value. What is your level of personal integrity? What is important to you? Look around for the true answers. Look at the details. Even your choice of clothing and music reveals your goals and how you feel about yourself.

You catch the blessing of the world when you see the bright side of yourself and life. The higher we value ourselves, the closer we come to the light of God. Jesus said, "You are like light for the whole world" (Matthew 5:14). Be a light to your own path. Know yourself as light.

We Damage Ourselves by Hurrying

There is always plenty of time for the important things. You never get it all done — you can't! The mind always presents one more, then one more, and then one more thing to do.

Stop! You have control of your Being, one step at a time. You have the final say. Put the brakes on or you will wreck your life emotionally.

We hurry too much. Your Being requires constant vigilance. Do not damage your value. We hold ourselves in high esteem when we relax and do not harm our preciousness. Do you scratch and dent your body, mind and soul? Stop, look and listen, just as you would if a speeding train were coming.

Slow Down with Meditation

Be faithful in your meditation. Despite its physical stillness, it is aliveness, not paralysis. Consciousness is awareness in action. You will have pierced the veil of illusion when you are here as pure light, pure consciousness, living in the moment.

When you feel scattered, sharpen your focus with slow, regulated breathing. When you are way out in left field, your breath goes wildly out of balance. Breathe deeply and slowly. Let your focus follow the breath. Be alert and aware of your breathing. There is a rhythm of the right nostril to the left. All day and night they shift. The body becomes ill when the rhythm of the nostrils gets out of balance.

Your breathing reflects your thinking. When meditating, the breath eventually slows. At the deepest level of meditation, the pulse also slows. This enables us to energize ourselves from within.

At the very deepest level, meditation resembles conscious hibernation. Yogis have been buried underground for months without air. So little is needed. You don't even need the heart to beat or to breathe.

When you contact eternity there is no time or space. Your body can sleep with your consciousness awake. This often occurs at night when you are neither asleep nor awake. Your breathing and pulse slow down, but you are still awake. During meditation you do not age because you are beyond time.

All great Masters have a similar expression and look in their eyes. They are of one family. They all have practiced and learned the proper breath.

Meditation Can Facilitate Memory

Slow the train of thoughts enough to look between the cars and see the blue sky. Thoughts are like white fluffy clouds in a blue sky. Focus on the sky and the clouds dissolve. What if you saw a Rolls Royce, a beautiful woman, or a child playing piano on that otherwise empty blue background? Would they not be easy to remember? If you saw only one of these, would it not be unforgettable?

When you increase awareness, you can remember more. When recalling a dream, you remember the images and pictures, not the words. You can remember anything when you transform words to pictures. Create visual images of objects in your mind. The more ridiculous, the easier to recall.

We relive our emotions as pictures. When feeling emotional about a person, we see that person in picture form. Dates, places and names can all be converted into pictures. Memory is a by-product of consciousness.

Mastery starts by using our minds and talents now. True meditation allows you to remember anything. A great wealth of information in the invisible world opens to you when you are responsible with your ordinary memory on a daily basis. The famous Frenchman, Comte de Saint-Germain, could compose and write two poems to two different people at the same time. This ability resulted from many years of meditation. He also perfected his memory and wrote a memory system book.

Open Your Heart

Enjoyment is a process of opening your heart. It goes along with self-esteem and self-value. Misery and suffering do not confer righteousness. You cannot enjoy happiness if you do not enjoy life now. It takes practice.

When we have self-esteem, we have a presence. We stop, look, listen and see the beauty and richness of life and the wonderful place we live in. We enjoy music, friends, health and comfort.

Open your heart and you reveal the most precious thing. The open heart has no space for darkness, only light. Renounce suffering and all that is miserable and unworthy.

The Kingdom of God is within. The heaven and earth worlds impregnate one another. Focus clear vision on your own goals, and you will not see error in others. You will be too busy enjoying the gifts of this life to condemn and impoverish yourself.

Ask Your Heart Your Questions

Your practical side weighs the pros and cons. The heart gives the "yes" or "no." Decisions come from that quiet part within. This is a paradox. You make decisions without making decisions. The "yes" feels right with a deep knowingness.

Any decisions we need to make about money, love, life, children or whatever call for going within to our quiet heart and listening to our intuition. When we go within the silence, we are free from worry and anxiety.

This life becomes so easy when we cut out the chatter. Let your heart guide you. Ask it your questions. Listen in silence for its answer.

Listen for the Yes or No

When opportunity comes, do you say "yes" or do you hesitate? Listen to your heart. If the answer is "yes," move toward the opportunity without doubt. Any other answer means "no," so act decisively and accordingly.

"Dummy doubt! The man who knows himself and the laws of cause and effect never doubts. He knows what he can do and what, for the moment, he cannot do," Peter insists. Simply concentrate on the do-able. The rest just drains your energy.

Be Authentic and Unashamed

Are you truly an authentic Being? If so, you do not need approval from others. Be authentic with yourself. Know that you have room for improvement and can expand as you work on yourself.

You only see clearly when you have the Light or are enlightened. To have the Light is to walk the highway to the Divine. It requires commitment.

The heart of the Divine encompasses all of us. God can mend any broken heart, but you must first bring all the pieces, all your troubles, into the sanctuary of God's meeting place in your heart. Listen and you find all your answers. There is no other gateway but through your divine heart.

God Is Now Here

We can either say, "God is no where" or we can say, "God is now here." It's simply a matter of where we break the letters to create the words that create our beliefs that create our activities that create our reality.

God is in the heart. God is now here. Not in the future or the past. We are not wandering generalities. We are statements of truth. The energy that fills all of us is what we call God.

God is in the pause, the sacred, silent place in our hearts. God can only be here now when we drop thoughts of the future and the past. The center is always calm. When we are calm, everything changes.

Let Divine Love Catch You

The romance of life is in falling in love with yourself for the very first time and knowing there is no going back. When you do, you find no "you" or "me," only

God. Be born to the new self that has always been there. When Divine Love catches you, you are helpless in Her hands.

The spring, summer, autumn and winter of your life involve sharing the wisdom of these stages. When you open your heart, the Divine will catch you and the new way occurs. You will see the gift you are here to bring. You are not complete until you accomplish what you have come to do.

Negativity Dies from Lack of Attention

Being around negative people can weigh you down, but if you keep your energy up you can excel and get stronger. Empty your cup of a lifetime by simply saying the past doesn't matter. If something hasn't helped so far, chances are it still won't. Truthfully examine your experiences.

Use the law of substitution. Moment by moment we can change old habits by acknowledging what makes us feel bad and choosing to substitute new behaviors, thoughts and images. This adds up to a new life.

The work to be done is done inside. We can't escape. We all want to be the chosen few. So choose to do the work.

Free Yourself from Clutter

You start collecting physically, mentally and emotionally, and before long you don't know what you've got. Ask yourself, "Does this really have value?" Free yourself of clutter. Chuck it! Be a contributor instead of a collector.

Do the same thing mentally and with unexamined belief systems. List your priorities. Look at your "to do" list that you feel so pressured to accomplish. Now, let's say you get a call from a special friend who offers to fly you, all expenses paid, to a most intriguing island. How many things on your "to do" list would you even care about? Which are irrelevant? Which are essential?

Determine the really important things and get them done. Let the rest go.

Clear out the clutter and your mind and body roll along harmoniously without jolting, hurried events. Allow your life to be a flowing melody, instead of marching to a 4/4 beat. The music of life is in the spaces between the notes. Allow spaces between the activities in your life. What is really important? The spaces between thoughts are your tickets to peace and joy.

We Think in Colors

We express our dominant mood or thoughts in the colors that we most frequently wear. When light hits an object, there is a radiation and vibration of sound and color. The color resonates with the different energy centers of the physical and spiritual body.

Thoughts are vibrations. Your dominant thought pattern is also your dominant auric color. Different thoughts radiate different colors, intensified by our emotions. We manifest these colors in our auric field and the clothes we choose.

Psychological characteristics are determined by the size of the corona, or the electrical field of the aura. We are fed by light, so black, dark or gray colors indicate emptiness or sadness. When angry, the aura is a smoking red or has clouds of black. If one is habitually angry, the aura looks dark. Cells will not grow in areas surrounded by black clouds. We feel a lack of life force in those areas. If you are experiencing confused thinking, don't wear plaids, confusing colors or busy patterns.

Green is a healing color with lots of heart. That's why the forest is so healing. Wearing higher octave colors allows you to feel better. This is not an issue of good or bad. It just is. When you wear lighter shades you feel better. People tend to worship everything but life. Choose what is life-promoting, not dead and depressing. Choose subtle hues that are light, airy and up.

Your House Is Filled with Thoughts

Houses are filled with thoughts and expressions. Thought forms of years of dialogues impregnate the walls. The subconscious never misses a word. It has 100% recall, though it may get blocked at a cellular level. Be aware of what in your surroundings affects your subconscious mind.

What you feast your eyes upon has a vibrational effect on your life. Pleasant photos and pictures are fine, but we can fall prey to physical illness created by negative vibrations over time. All the reminders that say, "I failed" add nothing pleasant to your environment. Old memories can become diseases that kill you.

When choosing art, know the intent of the artist. Abstract art distorts the real and beautiful and expresses confusion. Paintings reflect the artist's philosophy and love. Early Christian painters were forbidden to paint the human face. Later, they often used mud/blood colors and distorted the faces to look as if the people had glandular problems. Peter says, "Legend has it when the new thought age comes old art like this will disappear and we'll return to the grandeur and glory of art like that of ancient Athens that expressed worship of human excellence and perfection."

Do not allow images of depravity into your mind. Choose the literature you read as carefully as you choose pictures and art for your home. These create feelings, and what you feel is what you create. Let what entertains you be life-affirming. When traveling stay in non-smoking rooms. Stay clear of places that have the death smell and are nauseating.

Certain literature describes violence in a heroic context that inspires you to feel triumph, courage and hope. This differs from senseless violence with no courageous uplift or moral justification. Focus on literature with noble themes.

Have a light, bright bedroom and home that calls in light, bright vibrations. Send the melody of life and blessings, not death and addictions, into the spheres.

Your Objects Express Your Life

Take 15 minutes to assess the rooms you work and live in, paying particular attention to your sleeping room. What kind of vibrations and magnetism do you have in your personal environment? What colors and sounds surround you? Colors and sounds either heal or debilitate.

How do you feel about life? Look at what pictures are on the walls. If you need to, take them down and replace them. Get rid of anything unpleasant in your surroundings. Go through your home and sell, give away or discard anything that does not resonate melodiously for you. Dispose of the negative past before it kills you.

Find the Fulcrum of Your Pendulum

When we start being attentive, we can feel like we're on the end of a pendulum. When first picked up and released, a pendulum swings from one extreme to the other. One day can be like heaven and another day like hell.

The secret is to not get on the end of the pendulum. Be on top of the fulcrum. Find your calm center. If you live on the end of the pendulum, you are likely to be thrown off. Move into the center, where you can remain calm in the eye of the hurricane. When you sense an emotional storm coming, open the door and climb deep into your inner sanctuary. To do this you must know what this sanctuary smells, looks and feels like. Learn to identify your paradise.

Peace is your most valuable possession. If you allow a thought to steal your peace, get rid of it. Give your mental self something else to focus on. Peace calls for laser focus, like the sunbeam so focused through a magnifying glass that it burns.

Nothing Is as Permanent as Change

Embrace change as if it were stability. Get comfortable with change. When you can see permanence in change you are secure.

The Wheel of Life in the Tarot goes around and around. If you are in the center of life you are not tossed about. You're not in the mud if you're at the hub. The mud is flung off from the edges of the wheel.

In the center, we are not addicted to seasons or places. The wise Sage says, "When it is hot, I say it is hot, and when it is cold, I say it is cold, and I don't ask for it to be different." Where you are is where you are, and it is perfect. When you are centered, change is fine.

Focus on Your Goal

We all need visions, goals and dreams. Know what you are working toward. When you have no direction, life feels like sleep deprivation. To feel rested, useful and alive, couple your action with your vision.

Focus your resources in one direction, the way an Olympic athlete trains for an event. The gold medal is the symbol of a one-pointed mind. The step-by-step journey to your goal is an exhilarating gift.

We must have a goal. When focused, our consciousness infinitely expands at the speed of light, just like the universe. When we have a goal, we feel like we are stationary in time because we ride along with the universe. We are at peace wherever we go, because we are here now. This journey is exquisite!

Project Yourself Out 20 Years

Imagine that nothing can stop you from achieving your goals and fulfilling your desires. Then ask yourself:

- What would I do?
- Where would I live?
- With whom would I share my life?
- How much money would I have?
- What would I do with it?
- How would I help my friends?
- How much would I weigh?
- How athletically skilled would I be?
- How many musical instruments could I play?
- How many languages would I speak?
- How old would I look?

Put it on paper. Make a commitment to it. Sign, date and keep it where you can see it. When you see it, ask yourself what you may do today to arrive at that point. After you set twenty year goals, set ten, then five year goals. Then break them down to three year goals. Your three year goals keep you on track for your five, ten and twenty year goals and they are more immediate, so you focus on what you do annually. After you set one year goals, break them down to six month, three month and one month goals. Then to weekly and daily goals. Remember, what gets measured gets done.

Replace the Thoughts You Don't Like

To focus, you can only hold one thought at a time. Replace unpleasant thoughts with pleasant ones. Pleasant thoughts lead to a pleasant life. Meditate with life. Sit down now and then, and enjoy it. Don't gobble life down — savor it.

Pleasant thoughts have spaces between them more potent than the thoughts themselves. Those spaces are spirit. In the peaceful space between the thoughts, a cape of light is placed on your shoulders.

How to Change Any Ugly Behavior

We get locked into our habits. Even street people may get comfortable living in boxes. Fear of change paralyzes them, and they stay there. Before we can change negative behaviors we must eliminate selfishness and irritation.

Laziness is one form of selfishness. You don't have to feel guilty. Simply recognize your selfish, lazy habits and do something about them. Greed is another expression of selfishness. One form of greed is seeking others' approval. How far do you go for approval?

The irritated person judges himself unworthy. He needs a certificate of authenticity. To seek approval on the outside is futile when you haven't given yourself approval. Learn positive self-talk such as: "I can, I will and I am. I don't need to worry about anyone else's approval." A chronically irritated person's auric field is full of static. Static auric energy often results in skin rashes or sores on the body that won't heal.

Lack of humor builds our anger and irritation. If we are light-hearted, we easily laugh at ourselves and with others.

How Do You Want to Live?

If you want to be free, embrace thoughts of freedom. If you want to be happy, embrace thoughts of happiness. Be happy instead of right. You don't have to defend yourself — just step aside.

Jesus noted that one road leads to life and the more traveled road leads to death. When we come to a road less traveled, it truly is a super highway or "high way" to go.

Now is the time to make goals. How do you want to live? How are you going to live? The answer: "Any way I choose." Ask yourself, "What will enhance my original peace today?" Maybe to enhance your peace today would be to do nothing. You don't have to defend your choice — just step aside.

Spiritual abundance results from choosing to not continue doing what makes us feel lousy. This is not so simple when we get caught up emotionally. Emotions are the children of our thoughts. Thoughts can become patterns and habits. When you think lovingly, the results are self-evident. Don't just think positively; take positive action.

Renounce Addictions

Addictions become magnets for life experiences. When you renounce your addictions, you can get on with your glorious and luminous life. Suffering stinks. Renounce being sad and refuse to feel bad. Renounce your emotional demands of security, sensation and power. Do not apologize for wanting good things. Just be willing to do what it takes to get them. Addiction is the problem, not the desire.

Renounce complaining. It gives you headaches. Complainers deserve their lot in life. To get ahead, just do a little extra. Those who do just enough march in place with the herd. They are not Heroes of Light.

The secret to prosperity, health and bliss is surrender. When you surrender, you do so to God, and it is deep and blissful. Your heart sings a new song, and you find a deep abiding peace. You live in the land of milk and honey, the Kingdom of God within you.

Get into Good Habits

Sometimes it takes a long time to reverse the momentum of struggling with life. It takes only 21 days to establish a good habit or break a bad one. Just start. If you mess up, begin again. Be relentless in creating good habits.

This relentlessness creates the commitment you need to have the energy to change an existing habit. To quit the habit of smoking, have the energy to powerfully turn away. It takes energy to not put another cigarette in your mouth.

You need focused commitment to change any habit. You can't ride two horses at one time. Ask yourself, "Am I living in harmony and with purpose?"

Begin by charting your own negative behaviors. Then set clear, feasible goals to convert them to positive behaviors. By the inch it's a cinch, by the yard it's hard.

Next, thoughtfully visualize your new self-image. Use your imagination to see yourself as you want to be and your will to change your behavior. Then you'll win what you desire.

If you smoke and want to quit, don't get philosophical. Imagine you are smoke-free, and then don't stick it in your mouth. One hour at a time, let the habit die. To lose weight, imagine yourself slender and vital. Then stop eating as much as you do and exercise.

Discover what helps you feel good about yourself. Use it to bolster self-esteem. Excel discreetly and reinforce your self-esteem.

Chapter 3

Vitality

"Evolved beings who find life to be an exhilarating
pleasure seek the excitement of being as alive
and conscious as possible."
— Peter Rosen

The Outside Reflects the Inside

When you know your truth is inside, you know you are free. As you evolve, you learn that the truth is often not what you thought. Sometimes it's the opposite. Do you hold any beliefs that are the opposite of what you used to believe?

What's inside is reflected outside, and what's inside does come out. Squeeze an orange and you get orange juice. When you're squeezed under stress and pressure, how do you behave? It can only come out if it's on the inside first. The physical form is the container of your true essence. Your true essence reveals itself in your daily life.

A researcher at Yale University determined that our bodies are worth $6,524,000 instead of the commonly stated 98 cents worth of carbon and water. Certain hormones would be worth 6 million dollars a gram, and DNA is beyond valuation. The body is an incredible expression of our inner light.

Fresh and Raw Foods Energize Us

Fresh, raw, healthy, clean food strengthens the body. What goes in, comes out. We live on magnetism and vibrations, so we lower our energy by taking in over-processed foods we can't use efficiently. Higher life-force food helps us attain higher magnetism. Foods with vitality carry more charge.

A cell does not actually eat. Healthy cells have a positive and negative charge that creates magnetism. We eat for electromagnetic stimulation. The electromagnetic stream of energy is like a river flowing, turning a large mill wheel that produces power.

Green vegetation, such as sprouts, has a powerful electromagnetic field. Green leaves pull energy directly from the sun. Plants grow by converting sunlight. Solar power creates a vibration and this creates tremendous energy. Plants assimilate the same things we do, but more directly. Raw and fresh foods are incredibly high in enzymes and electromagnetic charges that stimulate and insulate the cells of the body. This electromagnetic charge is very important, because our thoughts are electromagnetic.

Chlorophyll has a potent electromagnetic charge. Chlorophyll is similar to hemoglobin — only the central atoms of the molecule differ. Chlorophyll has magnesium, whereas hemoglobin has iron. Magnesium in chlorophyll changes to iron in the human body, which helps build rich blood. Swishing fresh chlorophyll in the mouth keeps teeth and gums healthy by changing saliva pH balance to alkaline.

An exceptionally healthy diet would be gradually increasing chlorophyll consumption to 4 to 6 ounces in the morning, a salad in the afternoon and fresh foods in the evening, with an occasional cooked dish. Fresh and raw foods restore our bodies to their proper alkaline balance. The optimal target is to eat 90% fresh and raw foods. When we do eat cooked foods, those baked by the sun are highest in energy value. All foods affect our thought patterns.

It is fun to splurge on the occasional vegetarian pizza, even with a bit of cheese. For health reasons and because animals are their friends, many people choose not to eat meat. Eating foods with low-energy electromagnetic fields creates sluggishness.

There is magnetism of earth and magnetism of the above. When there is greater magnetism from above than below, you walk lightly upon the earth. Other days you may plod and pound the earth beneath you. Light-filled, energizing food lightens us.

Vegetarianism and Life Foods

Be neutral about your diet at first. Be less nervous and demanding of yourself and others. When your heart says not to eat meat, you will know. There is no right or wrong. Listen to your heart. It will tell you what to eat.

You have to ask yourself if what you eat fits your consciousness. All living things have a sensitivity, including plants. The caring person loves himself enough not to put anything in the body that is not working for him. It is worse, however, to judge someone who does eat meat than to consume it yourself. Jesus said, "It is not what goes into a person's mouth that makes him unclean, but what comes out of it that makes him unclean" (Matthew 15:11).

If you are allergic to certain foods, you feel a mental aversion to them. When stressed or insecure, the immune system cannot tell a friend from a foe. It gets confused, or we ignore our aversion, and a physical allergic reaction occurs.

When you are deeply happy and at peace, allergies dissipate. Liver cleansing and attitude cleansing help balance the immune system. Listen to your body to learn the foods with the highest vital force for you.

You can use muscle testing to determine the most vibrant foods for you. Ask someone to help. Lie down, and place a food on your solar plexus. Stretch out your arm, and ask the other person to try to push your arm down as you try to lift it. Try this with several foods. Ask the other person to determine how your resistance level varies with different foods, perhaps using a numeric scale from one to five. The higher your resistance, the better the food for you. Which foods are most appropriate for your health? Which foods decrease your energy?

How You Eat Shows How You Live

How can some people eat so much and some people so little? Eating often has to do with addiction. "I need" is rooted in fear and survival. People with this fear of living will keep eating though no energy results. You can tell much about a person based on how he relates to food. Food and money operate similarly. It's your feelings about them that count.

You require very little food when you are filled with spirit. A healthy body weight and size can be maintained on very little food consumption. If you eat a balanced diet primarily composed of raw and fresh foods, 1100 to 1200 calories per day can nourish you quite well. You could even gain weight on those few calories, because your system is clean and efficient.

Food Intake and Longevity

Clive McKay conducted a study at Cornell University on rats that demonstrates the relationship between food intake and longevity. When the rats ate one-half their usual daily portions, they lived about twice as long. Morris Ross of the Institute for Cancer Research in Philadelphia, Pennsylvania found that mice lived 60% longer when given half the usual portions.

Low calorie intake increases longevity. A study of tokophyra, a carnivorous micro-organism, found their life span increased 800% when they cut back from all day continuous feedings to twice a day.

Many people interested in health don't know how to eat, so they eat too much. Smaller food volume leads to less corrosion on the poles of the cells. You have more energy and don't accumulate extra fat.

Balance your attitude and your appetite. You need less food when you have less worry and frustration in your life. Major worries can burn up to 6,000 calories a day.

Metabolism and Respiration

It has been suggested that humans may have a fixed metabolism rate at 80 million calories per pound in proportion to body weight over a lifetime. Shortly after consuming that much, they die. Perhaps there are even a certain amount of breaths genetically allotted for a lifetime. Breathing and food intake are connected.

When the body is in tune, the calorie intake decreases. This is nature's way of decreasing the need for respiration. As you regulate your breathing you regulate your attitude. Change your breathing, and you change the way you think. You breathe most efficiently when you are relaxed.

Sugar and Fat

The likelihood of inducing cancer in laboratory rats increases when they are fed extremely high fat diets. We are tremendously talented in preparing and creating high fat savory foods and desserts.

Many people speed up the aging process by eating rancid fats loaded with sugar. Fresh and raw foods burn slowly, like hard wood, and produce lots of heat without much smoke. Fats, like soft or medium wood, burn without a lot of heat. Protein, like wet pine, smolders without much heat, but with lots of smoke and creosote. Animal protein takes a long time to go through the human digestive system, because we don't have short colons (like carnivorous animals) that process it quickly before it putrefies. People like to eat meat because of the taste, which really comes from poisons in the meat. Eating meat is eating all the toxins left in the dead animal.

We do need some proteins and sugar in our diet, but we must choose them carefully. We get tired when we eat too much bread or too many crackers. If eating cheese, do so in small proportion. Vegetable proteins are better, but we need to combine them with certain enzymes. Sugar operates like a New York taxi driver, racing you around until you drop. When used in moderation, honey has certain therapeutic value. It is still a sugar, and because it is good for you doesn't mean a lot is better than a little.

Observe the Effects and Decide

Your body will speak to you if you will listen. Be aware of how you feel prior to eating something, and then how you feel after eating it. When we are toxic our breath smells. We have no body odor when we are healthy — our feet don't stink, we don't need deodorant, and our breath smells sweet.

Cleaner foods cause less toxicity. When we eat foods cooked at temperatures even as low as 108-118 degrees many enzymes are killed. Even the most hardy enzymes die at 130 degrees. If one is going to eat a lot of heavy cooked foods and junk foods, then extraordinary means must be taken to stay healthy. Super Oxide Dismutase (SOD) is one supplement that can help maintain a state of health. SOD is such an effective antioxidant that it can flourish inside nuclear reactors.

If vitamins make you feel better, use them — but don't worship them. Vitamin C helps heal the cellular structure. Cells may have limited times they can double, perhaps up to 50 times, before they die. Some researchers say vitamin E can increase this limit to 120 times. The longer you keep a cell healthy, the longer you live.

When Eating, Be in Grace

Your thoughts produce the digestive juices that mix with saliva and become part of your body. Your thoughts shape your body. Do not discuss problems while eating, or you will poison yourself. Have positive conversation.

Be grateful while you eat. Be prayerful, not so much with words as with love and appreciation. Appreciation makes you a superb alchemist. Great appreciation can change poison into nectar and lack of appreciation can turn nectar into poison.

When you have tremendous gratitude for the food you eat, you fill quickly. Fill up with thankfulness for the food you have been given until tears fill your eyes.

Graciousness is the ease of movement that allows you to flow effortlessly in this life. Your gratitude and relaxed grace while eating result from luminous thought, which puts you in touch with the light. Be grateful, and you need no other meditation. When you get to this point, you transmute the food to its source, light. Live in grace and with gratitude for what you have.

Beliefs and the Body

Your hands, eyes, face and the way you gesture are signatures of your beliefs, thoughts and emotions. Thoughts in the brain create emotions in the body. For example, look for constricted pupils in the eyes of people who feel angry at limitation in their lives. The Sufi say, "You look like you feel and think." Below are some physical indicators of certain character traits, thoughts and beliefs.

Hands and Fingers

The hands represent our life. The balanced hand is neither stiff or loose.

Thumb: Signifies the head, particularly the pineal gland, pituitary, and hypothalamus. A person with a very strong, long, thick thumb is incredibly persistent. He sees and likes to do things his way.

Index or Jupiter finger: Indicates joy and dealings with others. Long index fingers indicate leadership, for good or bad. If too long and thick, leadership may be out of balance.

Middle or Saturn finger: Represents the mysteries of life, including philosophy. An extraordinarily long middle finger may indicate a lot of turmoil or a tendency to brood.

Ring or Apollo finger: Environment, home and decoration. A gold ring worn on this finger increases harmony with environment.

Little or Mercury finger: Communication, family, finances and sexuality. When there is a wide spread between the little finger and the ring finger or the little finger is way out, there is a tendency to be impulsive and to act quickly. When the little finger curves in, the person is adept at sales or doing business.

Shorter fingered people are doers. A farmer's hands are often square-palmed, with shorter, thicker fingers.

Pointed fingers represent sharp and quick people. Longer fingered people need more quiet time. Thinkers have very long fingers. Musicians, readers and librarians often have long, slender hands, especially if they love their work. These people may be prone to emotional storms.

Fingers that bend back indicate a tendency to bend backwards to please.

The round palm signifies fluidity. This person cooperates smoothly with others.

Knuckles: Well developed knuckles indicate hesitation in thought. This person thinks more before he acts. The tips of the fingers carry a lot of energy when we talk. We can emphasize points and send energy by touching different fingertips together.

Each finger has three flanges. The flange closest to the palm signifies the physical realm; the second, the mental; and the third at the tip of the fingers, spiritual.

The two middle fingers closest together indicate that the person may be concerned with environment, philosophy, and/or have some concern with money issues. If on the right hand only, the problem is in the present. If on the left hand only, the problem is past. For the left-handed person, the past and future is reversed. To enhance prosperity, keep the middle fingers open. All fingers far apart say, "I'm open to almost anything." This person may be impulsive.

Nails: Square nails on the environment or ring finger reveal a more conventional person who likes things kept the same. Square fingernails on the index finger, the Jupiter finger which represents joy, indicates someone who is not very happy dealing with people and who does so with deliberation.

When we are uncomfortable about our life, we may hide our hands in our pockets.

How do you use your hands? Keep your hands flexible, not floppy. Hands are like the tail a dog wags to stimulate electromagnetic fields. This is true with the bottom of the feet as well. There are secondary energy centers in the hands and feet.

Rings: Wearing a diamond on the small finger enhances communication skills, processing financial issues, selling your ideas to partners and employers, and sexual communication skills. A diamond worn on the ring finger reinforces your environment. Wearing a diamond on the middle finger reinforces religion and philosophy. Wearing one on the index finger strengthens your interaction with other people and enhances your directing skills.

Eyes

The fiber structure of the iris of your eye indicates your health potential. If the fibers are firm and straight, you have more potential for vitality. If the fibers are further apart or crooked, you need to use conscious awareness to take care of yourself. Strong and tight fiber structures indicate a capacity to endure fairly abusive daily rituals. This person endures like an oak table, rather than the easy-to-split pine.

Faces

A round face has nothing to do with weight. This person finds it easier to be with people and will roll with situations.

The square-faced person is more fixed and often seen as stable. He dislikes a lot of movement and doesn't roll easily. He likes established roots.

Triangular face (broader at the brow) indicates a more adventuresome person who perceives, analyzes and moves quickly. He usually has sharp features.

Someone involved with finance, such as a banker, often has a heavier area between the ear and the back of the cheek, kind of like a chipmunk. He does not necessarily have a strong jaw. He accumulates things.

The elongated face indicates interest with more non-material issues.

A strong jaw structure indicates a very determined person.

A strong nose signifies a person willing to encounter obstacles. If it is big and turned down some, he has much drive and motivation. A nose turned down too much indicates a tendency to be too critical.

Over time, listening to music can change the size and shape of our ears to hear the sounds better.

The Electric, Magnetic Body

People who live together start to think alike and this changes their physical structure. Our thoughts create our electric energy field.

Be extremely aware of what your fingers and hands are doing. The hands vibrate with a lot of energy. We talk with our hands and fingers, especially during a handshake when the energy centers come together in a clasp of friendship. In prayer we put them together for an exchange of energy.

Healing occurs when we pull things out of the auric field with the magnets of our hands. Healers who use touch rinse their hands in cool, running water after working with illness or injury because running water neutralizes by pulling off the positive ion charges.

Posture and Personality

Change your posture and you'll change your personality, or change your attitude and watch your posture shift. The body does not lie. It expresses how you feel at the moment. It can also change with awareness. Strength and endurance develop when you are true to yourself. Athletic endeavors always return 1000% because they increase positive self-esteem.

People with back problems usually carry heavy loads emotionally. Their shoulders, back or knees collapse. Your load lightens when you are flexible. To counter rigidity, do flexibility exercises. Move with grace and ease. Build your pectoral muscles to feel more comfortable and outgoing. Or change your attitude and your pectorals will build. Developing the back muscles increases the tendency to be reserved.

Leg strength helps you stand your ground. Do leg squats to build your legs and reinforce stability and balance in your life. When we gain physical balance we also gain mental balance and vice versa. When you walk, feel your feet touch the ground. Frustrated, angry people have a hard, heavy walk. People who are out of touch with reality tip-toe.

Trusting in the universe gives you mental balance, so you walk in a balanced and easy, yet directed, manner. The open life is more relaxed. Buddha said, "Kings walk like kings because they are." If you remember that life is a sacred privilege, you will fill with gratitude and move in grace. Remember that to live in grace, you must move with grace.

Chapter 4

Prosperity

"You must be rich inside first,
if outer richness is to have any meaning.
You will only become rich outside
by enriching the lives of others."
— Peter Rosen

Prosperity Mirrors Your Way of Being

Prosperity is not difficult. Learning how to be loved is difficult. If you feel worthy of love you can accept money. If you feel loved by the universe, prosperity flows to you magically. People who feel loved work with joy.

Make doing your job a pleasure, not a burden. To be prosperous you must either love what you do or change jobs. Find something enjoyable about your work and see it as a game or challenge. Enlightened people love to work. Great bliss occurs when you put forth great energy. Practice what you love.

The boss represents a parent relationship. Our employers become our substitute parents and issues of being loved or not loved surface in our relationships with them. Learn what you can from them.

Collectors of money force themselves to work hard to get and keep money. You will either spend your life working for money or having money work for you. Your attitude determines your choice.

Prosperity Is an Attitude

Prosperity results from this attitude: "I want to serve my customer because it brings me great satisfaction." When we find the best in ourselves, we serve people. Profit results. Without profit, we cannot stay in the business of providing our services. Give your customers what they want, and they will help you increase your prosperity. You go into business to profit so you can continue the process. Through this you provide a valuable service.

If you don't want to be the best at what you do, get out of it or change your attitude. You must like what you do. If you enjoy a hard task, it doesn't make you suffer, it makes you happy. Look for one new constructive step in your work each day. Be willing to take responsibility for getting the job done. If you don't get a raise from that employer, you will get an offer from another one. People remember the little things you do.

When you find the best in yourself, you can find the best in everyone else. If you look for excellence and service in people, you bring it out in them. Good business management is loving people.

When you find out what is right, keep doing it. The wrong will fall away. You will have more opportunities than you can dream of, plus more money and more friends. Choose. Although you would like to do it all, you'll have to stick to your purpose and say "no" to some things.

Your expectation creates your attitude. You generally get what you expect. What you expect manifests.

If you complain, you expect bad things to happen and they do. Pursue peace and happiness by doing something you love. When you pursue what you enjoy, you have no time to be sad and depressed. You are too busy enjoying yourself.

Learning from mistakes builds stepping stones to your next victory. The past propels you into the future. Be the best shepherd of your abilities and desires. Then watch prosperity unfold.

Poverty or Prosperity

"Poverty is not determined by the clothing one wears. Poverty is a hollow hunger that can never be filled, it is an abyss, a bottomless pit, a grand gorge of greed. Hell is never having enough. That's what poverty is all about. An empty stomach is easy to fill, but an empty soul is difficult to satisfy. For one, bread is all that is needed, but for the other, an everlasting spirit is required. We need both."*

You will not succumb to poverty if you are not anxious, apprehensive, depressed or afraid. These attitudes confuse thought. You need to clearly discern between the true and the false.

Prosperity consciousness means you are happy and experiencing pleasure now.

Manifesting Prosperity

Believe you deserve to have good things. "Money is not the answer, nor is it the problem. It is only a comfort, and who of us would be so selfish as to greedily begrudge another for enjoying such a simple convenience?"*

Living well involves intention and the application of energy. Life can become an exhilarating game when we concentrate our energy. When we learn to concentrate, we do not lack richness of spirit, health, laughter or money.

Over the next thirty days, determine to do whatever you do at such levels of excellence that not one thing will be left undone. Your life will change. You will probably get a raise. If not, the universe will reward you.

There Is No Such Thing as Scarcity

Do not limit money with impoverished thoughts. Quit believing in scarcity. Quit believing there is not enough stuff to go around.

When we are young, we are often taught to believe in scarcity in the form of the idea that "they have it all and we don't have enough." This belief leads to an expectation that life is limiting and teaches us to blame others because they have what we do not.

There Is More Than Enough

If, as a baby, you thought there was not enough milk, you quickly learned that there was not enough stuff in this world. Hearing throughout childhood that others have what we don't perpetuates our belief in scarcity. An attitude of hating the rich may develop. Resentment of others who have money keeps us poor. You cannot believe that wealth in monetary form is evil and expect to manifest prosperity.

"A man becomes rich, not by mistake nor by stealing from others. He becomes rich because he enriches the lives of others first. We should never resent success in others. Rejoice and celebrate in others' success. For some, this may appear difficult, and yet, this is an overlooked universal law. You will never be successful until you love success in others."*

This life is magical unless you have a suffering mentality, which comes from the perpetuated lie that you aren't worth much. Do not hold a suffering-is-blessed mind set. The world will whip you if you believe you're not worth anything. Do not believe in a limited supply, because if there's a limited amount you can't enjoy what you have. You can't be generous if you fear. You feel small and without influence if you have nothing to share with another.

People are poor because they think poorly. There will always be a redistribution of wealth. Money will always flow to the rich because poor people have the wrong attitude toward money. Their attitude is a violation of the universal law of opulence.

God is abundant love, life, light, opulence and joy.

"Needy" Is a Violent Word

If we are anti-profit we are pro-loss. You cannot give your services and goods away free and earn a profit. Without profit, the work force eventually gets cut back and pretty soon there is a big parade of people going down the street who want a handout. Ironically, these needy people think that the merchant who doesn't give a handout is greedy and just out for a profit.

When people say, "We need," they usually want the government to do it for them. But the government eventually can't give everything that people want. Governments frequently split into two factions, one for profit and one for handouts, and start fighting. Chaos results. Then the masses say, "Burn it down." When this demand manifests in revolt, other governments get into the barroom brawl, and wars occur. In religions, when the Master says, "I can't feed you all," the revolt begins.

When we try to solve neediness through government, eventually those who receive feel victimized because they never have enough. The curse of accepting the unearned is that it reveals an emptiness of soul. Every act of accepting the unearned is a stinging reproach against what is left of integrity. People who seek the unearned become desperate. When all the neediness cannot be met, the recipients rebel, and the crash occurs.

It's over because we became "needy." History provides lessons because the fundamental principles remain the same. A wealthy country doesn't destroy itself until sufficient people are against wealth. Owners of beautiful homes do not jeopardize themselves or their homes for anti-profit ideals.

The more you require of a government, the more you create a dictator. The end result of freebies is dictatorship. Whenever we are anti-profit we are pro-loss, and everyone loses. This is the process that destroys civilizations.

Eradicate Poverty

We all make a difference, every one of us. If we want to eradicate poverty in the world, we must not be impoverished ourselves. If we want to eliminate strife, we must first be in peace.

We all make a difference. It is our duty to be prosperous and self-sufficient. Then at least we are not a burden. The solution starts with us, and through education that teaches marketable skills. When our heart fills with compassion, we are not closed to others. Educating others is the most valuable gift.

It is proper to have wealth and live well. This is contrary to some churches in both the East and West that promote poverty. Many teachings of Christ have been misunderstood, and people have suffered and felt guilt unnecessarily. We deserve the best, and the best is yet to come.

Money Is Only a Servant

Most people spend their life looking at their yearning power instead of their earning power. Life must be more than yearning. It must have action, or your dreams are fruitless.

King Solomon understood wealth and what it could do. He built a great temple by drafting men in rotating crews of 10,000, and then inviting the best craftsmen to oversee the work. God promised to live in the temple when Solomon finished it. Solomon knew that materialism brings us nothing until we infuse it with the spirit that comes through our work.

When money results from our thoughts and actions, we have earned it. The truly wealthy are free of guilt, because they know happiness comes with creation. They aren't addicted to the wealth of the outcome.

To a powerful and wealthy man, a yacht is only a yacht. Enjoy it, that's what it's for. No one can enjoy it like the person who earned the money to buy it.

The truly rich person is rich with spirit and is not threatened by money. He is the Master of his universe, and money is only a servant in his home. We attract material goodness along with the growth of our inner goodness. We're from heavenly stock. Develop a built-in feature that expects good things to happen. God loves us as a father loves a child, without lack or limitation.

Keys to Opulence

Release poverty mentality. Let go of ideas about scarcity. Let go of ideas that someone took it away. Stop associating money with unpleasantness, such as having to work when you would rather play.

Affirm, "I enjoy what I do to earn money."

Make money at what you love doing. Write ten to twelve things you love doing, things you'd be willing to pay to do. Then write ten to twelve ways to make money doing them. Be for profit.

Apply playful effort. Create an energy of opulence, even if results are years away. The universe always pays.

The less often you get paid the more you get. Day laborers make the least. Those paid weekly earn slightly more. Those paid every two weeks earn more and those paid once a month more yet. The highest earners may be paid quarterly or once a year. Nobel prizes are paid once in a lifetime.

Don't be so serious about money.

Enjoy paying for what you receive in life.

Apply Excellence to Earn Money

To earn money, apply your own brand of excellence. Do this and you have it all. Your tastes and desires change and you start living in simple elegance.

As you apply your excellence you become more aware of, and content to watch, the sunrise and the sunset. You have mastery over your environment. When you operate in excellence, you focus on whatever you do. You have many talents. Use them one at a time. If you're certain something is good for you, it's twice as potent. Do that activity first.

Money Is Attracted to Love

Money is divine energy that is attracted to love. Expend energy in the pursuit of your joys and you will have it returned to you ten times, if not a hundred to a thousand times more than you give out. Try this exercise: Find someone worthy that you feel good about and give a certain amount of money to him. Give it out and in a week or so it will return ten times. Doing this is rational self-interest. Don't ever give out of guilt. Guilt is a negative magnet that repels any good thing coming to you. Guilt only attracts more guilt.

Give because your heart is so full that you have to give, for he who has the most love is the fittest in the world. Give as if you are a fruit tree so heavily laden with bounty that in giving you free your limbs to jump up toward the sun in eternal praise. Give what you have in complete faith that if you contribute to life then life will return the bounty. That's the way the system works. It is simple and daring. Everyone is invited to participate or procrastinate in the enjoyment of the blessings. When you give because you really want to give, the soil is so rich that seed money bears fruit.

Never close the door of your tender compassion for those who can truly benefit from your giving. The little things you do show how large you are. You can plumb the depths of someone's character by observing how he operates in surface events.

We live in a world of survival of the fittest, and he who has the most love survives.

We Always Do What We Want

Do not be sold on having a lousy life. If you keep doing what drains you, you will create an opportunity to slow down. The easiest choices come early on. If you wait until they're forced on you, you will have a tougher time.

Don't use your challenges as reasons not to act. Truth is simple. Decisions need to be made so that your life, health, comfort and peace are maintained.

Forget Past Money Mistakes

If you get heavy-handed about your falls in life and start on an analysis program over why this or that happened while continuing to lie there, you may get trampled by those getting on with their lives. To try and find reasons for your fall is often an excuse for giving up on life. A healthy person never finds anything of value when he digs through his archives of past negative experience. Learn from past mistakes and then drop them. Don't go back and dig up the dirt of the past. You create the future by what you do now.

Focus on what you did that was productive and satisfying and do more of it even better, now.

Be Productive and Happy

Choose to be happy and blissful and to live in ecstasy. Choose to create financial comfort through your effort. Happiness is the gateway to your enlightenment. Value who you are and find ways to embrace life.

To be happy, be here now. Renounce the past and let the future arrive when it does. Make decisions now that give you a financially secure and satisfying position in life. This simple attitude is magical.

It takes trust in yourself to do what you want. Trust doesn't mean being gullible, or doing or believing things without examination. Choose with awareness.

Never Too Old for a Career You Love

It is so sad to see laid-off workers in their forties or fifties say, "What can I do? I am too old." It is equally sad to live with fear of losing a job.

Keep up your marketable skills. What can you do that is in demand? Visualize, brainstorm, put your ideas on paper and begin.

Do the Opposite of All Limiting Acts

What do the poor do to stay poor? Figure that out, then do the opposite. Most of the poor work at jobs they do not find pleasurable. Some people use poverty as a way to get even with their parents, as if to say, "I'll make you take care of me." Others keep themselves poor when they have rich elderly parents because they don't feel they deserve their inheritance unless they are poor. They sabotage themselves.

King Solomon said, "As a man thinketh in his heart so he is." An evil lie that we are unworthy is the basis of our belief in our unlovableness. What we think in our heart, we visualize and feel. These pictures or images that we hold become our reality. We are the makers, not the servants, of our karma.

We create it all, so make sure you're creating what you want. Be limitless. Take obstacles as challenges. Don't give your peace away.

The Luminous Life

Your life will be luminous when you live with awareness. Give yourself permission to move fluidly through life in abundance. When it comes to money, you may choose to have a little or a lot, but you feel no lack whatsoever. Abundance does not necessarily mean a lot of money, but prosperity consciousness does mean that you can have everything you desire. True wealth is the ability to use the "I Am-ness" of your being to bring opulence to all.

A tree needs enough energy to bud, blossom and bear fruit. We too need enough energy inside us. What does an orchardman do with a barren, unproductive tree? He chops it down and uses it for firewood. People become barren when they insist on being sad. When others are too serious about life, we are uncomfortable in their company.

Spiritual Teachers are Models

If one can live luminously and successfully then there is hope for all to do so. Authentic spiritual teachers show us the way by being models.

Masters require us to embrace a profound questioning of truth. One of the laws is as Jesus said,

"To he who has, more shall be given" (Matthew 13:12). This law is based on an attitude of affluence.

A person with an abundant attitude does not beg in his prayers. Those who have eyes to see and ears to hear experience an abundant universe.

You Are Here to Blossom

When you are joyful you live abundantly. You are the fruit of life. You are here to blossom happily. If you do not produce and share your fruit, you, like the tree, begin to die. "To pass this life as an unopened blossom is a travesty. Unless you throw open the gates of your heart with both seed and petal impregnating the very earth, the perfume of your love will not rise to the altar divine."*

You are alive as long as you blossom and have something to share, but Peter insists, "the ones who give with their pocketbook and not their hearts have missed the whole point. People who do not share their riches, joys or gifts and accumulate much are like those who have a full cup of wine and do not drink of it for fear that the supply is limited. The air, in time, turns it to vinegar — their lives sour. Those who refuse to fill their cups from this spring of goodness forever remain thirsty and impoverished; their lives are dry and bitter."

When we dry up and there is nothing more in us, our creative juices stop flowing and we die. Produce the sweet and satisfying that brings you joy.

Rich Beggars

"This man's talk was 'How to Enjoy Being Rich,' yet his face and eyes revealed a haggard, tired look. That's a very subtle form of greed. If you always want more, then you never have enough. There is no difference between a rich beggar and a poor beggar — both feel that if they had more, they would be happy."*

There is a huge difference between "If I be more I'll have more" and "If I have more I'll be more." Many wealthy people are just rich beggars. Poor people are often preoccupied with money, but greedy and rich people are just as preoccupied. A bowl made of greed can never be filled. You have to be more first and then you'll have more. The natural process of life is abundance. If you are greedy, money becomes an issue, not an abundance.

"When we are non-addicted, free from greed, the crystal glass of our being is filled from an unending source. We give our richness so we may be filled again and again and again, eternally."*

Miserable People Have Miserable Philosophies

Don't cling. Especially don't cling to money. Peter says, "As long as you have even the slightest vestige of addiction to money, you will never use it wisely, nor will you have it multiply. Money is a seed that will grow an abundant crop as long as you are not constantly pulling it up to see if it is growing or not."

Have the courage to let go of ideas and limitations. Remember the processionary caterpillars. If you put an apple core in the middle of the group of processionary caterpillars and the leader goes in a circle around it, they all follow the leader, going around the apple core until they die of starvation. Let go of the limiting ideas that bind you. Your philosophy makes you happy or miserable. You can choose to see the world as perfect, or you can see and create discord.

Living Is an Art

If you want to go anywhere in this life, you will have to learn to say "thank you."

There are two types of people:

- Those who see perfection in the midst of discord.
- Those who see discord in the midst of perfection.

Those who see perfection while in discord and pain know that happiness skills are learned by doing.

"Heroes of life see fortune in the midst of misfortune, opportunity in the midst of what appears to be a most inopportune situation and light when everyone about them cries darkness."*

The World Is Peace and Happiness

Wherever we are is where peace is. Wealth is being rich wherever we are. A Master lives in another kingdom and is enslaved by nothing. Get rich, but don't be addicted to it or it will become your master. You choose the kingdom you want to live in. Do not judge others. Do not feel inadequate. Do not judge yourself.

Recognize Your Talent

You will always be a truly rich person if you recognize your talent. Talent is the way you view yourself and your performances. When you see yourself with excellence inside, you can master abundance outside. Be light about money. The visible reality is as much heaven as the invisible reality. It is all light, including money.

The Law of Enrichment

You only attain wealth in the long run by enriching the lives of others first. This is the law of enrichment. The universe rewards you when you are a faithful steward.

It is a spiritual law that when you serve and enrich others by bringing beauty, joy and comfort into their lives, an abundance of time, money, health and prosperity will seek you out.

The consensus is in. We know there are honest, decent, rich people.

Acres of Diamonds

Russell Conwell tells this true story in his book, *Acres of Diamonds*:

Al Hafed was looking for a way to make a fast fortune, so he left his farm to search for diamonds. An old priest asked Al why he wanted to do this. Al said he just had to search and seek.

After years of desperation and no diamonds, Al Hafed committed suicide.

Back on Al's old farm, the new owner took his camel to the oasis to drink one day. He looked down and saw some shiny black stones. He took one home and put it on the mantle. The old priest came by and saw the stone, and said that Al Hafed had searched for rocks like that. The priest thought it was a diamond. It was.

The farm Al Hafed left became the richest diamond mine in all the world.

Often we go searching for what we don't see right before us. We don't recognize the gifts we already have, because we get lost in the search.

Help the Country by Helping Yourself

Be the least dependent on outward circumstances as possible. How do you help the welfare system? By not being on welfare. Don't be dependent. Take care of yourself so others don't need to take care of you.

Be responsible. Do now what gives you peace and independence. Only an independent person can be truly healthy.

Department of Labor statistics show that ninety-seven out of one hundred people by age sixty-five will depend on social security to live. Do not depend on this system. The more self-sufficient you are, the fewer problems you'll have.

To believe you can succeed and be prosperous is a challenge for many. Life does have challenges, dangers and excitement, but life doesn't have to be difficult unless you believe it does.

There Ain't No Free Lunch

This is one of the profound "secrets" of the universe: Knowing there is no free lunch frees us.

Another secret of the universe is to be as free from debt as possible. Purchasing a house is an investment that for most will require a reasonable debt, but too many have the kind of debt that imprisons. Remember, you can invest in a home, or go in debt for a place to live.

Save money so that if tough times come you can pay off what you owe. When turmoil hits, you want to survive those times until prosperity returns. It will, as surely as the spring comes with its singing robins.

Some believe there will be a physical re-birth of our planet following the cleansing of the old. The earth is in the cleansing process now, for it has been sick for a long while. Part of the sickness of the earth is due to thought patterns we hold. Many hold the thought pattern that someone owes us something. Many believe that we can not run our own lives.

Procrastination is the fear of results. Get on with it. Go for the results you want. Start visualizing and feeling yourself as rich. The outer manifestation will follow.

Believe in Your Worth

Spirituality is not separate from prosperity, health or knowledge. You can change wealth patterns. Don't blame the universe. You are a co-creator of this prosperous universe. Begin by discovering you are a little more than just okay. Then the universe gives you more. Resentment, greed and anguish follow low self-esteem. As you think more securely, you create the circumstances of the life you choose to live. Money is neither the root of all evil, nor a cure-all. Money adds enjoyment of creature comforts. It is no crime to feel good. It is natural. Make yourself as healthy, prosperous and attractive as you can and you will feel great. This expresses and reinforces your self-esteem.

Say to yourself often, "I am worthy. I don't have to suffer and beg for my bread."

Action Earns Results

Money is a tool to be respected, not condemned. Your virtue creates money. Money is the outward effect of the highest in your Being, a wonderful servant that allows you to give and affect things thousands of miles away. Money can bring peace and comfort to your heart. Has poverty brought anyone happiness? Poverty holds no virtue.

You earn money by applying yourself virtuously to your higher values. Philosophy is great, but action earns results. Action is like earnest money. It shows that you are earnest. Apply a lot of virtue, and you'll earn a lot of money.

You may have been taught that money is wicked. Many translators of the Bible promoted poverty and powerlessness as a virtue, because people who believe they deserve nothing are easier to control.

Much of the Bible has been translated and retranslated through various languages, and finally a copy of a copy of a copy of a copy was accepted. The translators slanted the Bible to imply that money was the root of all evil. Perhaps these translators forgot about Joseph, Abraham, David, Solomon, Nicodemus, Joseph of Arimathaea and many other pillars of Biblical history who were very wealthy.

This heresy serves no one. The impoverished person may not help himself or others because he does not feel he has enough to give. Poverty may hold no virtue, but a poor person can be virtuous. Love yourself enough to do something good for yourself. Then you can help someone else.

If you had ten times the money you had right now, what would you do with it? What causes would you support? Use 10% of what you have now for those causes.

There is more than enough. You don't need to ask, "Can I afford it?" Instead, say, "The I Am that I Am creates more than I need." We are abundant Beings. Be virtuous, cheerful, diligent and persistent in what you do, and you will be showered with abundance.

For Peace & Prosperity

Ask yourself these three questions everyday. They are amazingly effective.

1. What enables peace and is best for me right now?

2. What one thing done excellently today would be the most important to my life?

3. What is the most difficult task that faces me today?

Do #3, then #2, then #1. Do the difficult first, get it over and done with. The difficult robs you of energy until it's done. Once your most difficult task is out of your way, you are free to use your energy for the most important thing. Choose the action right for the moment by choosing what enables peace and delivers important results.

PETER'S PROSPERITY TIPS

1. Let your close association be with only thankful, appreciative people, who know how to say "thank you," and ask nothing in return.

2. Never ever listen to the whiner or the complainer. If you do, you may begin to feel the world is unjust and unfair. The complainer throws hot coals into your eyes, and blinds you to the beauty and richness that is yours. Avoid them like the plague.

3. Associate only with people who follow through. Those whose word is their honor. People who do not do what they say, are dishonest. Dishonesty breeds poverty on all levels of being.

4. End each day by writing all the blessings you have incurred that day; all the reasons to say "thank you." You will sleep sweetly and richly. Your night will be continuous affirmation of prosperity.

5. Make beauty your god, and worship it in everything you see, feel and experience. Then your life will be beautiful, peaceful and rich. Remember, ugliness becomes beauty when you see the reason for contrast. The star shines brighter because the night is dark.

6. Do not envy others. For to do so is to only affirm your own lack. If you envy others, you are only saying "poor me." So be it . . . you have two wishes left!

7. Rejoice and celebrate in others' success. For some, this may appear difficult, and yet, this is another overlooked universal law. You will never be successful until you love success in others.

8. Let your self-talk be free of condemnation. Learn from your mistakes, and forget them. That's why pencils have erasers on them. If you focus on your so-called mistakes, remember, you get what you set!

9. Value time - spend it wisely. Don't allow others to steal it with trivia. Many people have lots of time, while other people have lots of money. The prosperous person has both.

10. You must be rich inside first, if outer richness is to have any meaning. You will only become rich outside, by enriching the lives of others. You will only become rich inside, when you can understand what real value is all about. Never confuse glass with diamonds . . . A few diamonds go a long way!

Chapter 5

Money

"Look for beauty and quality in everything.
Make beauty your god and worship it
in everything you see, feel and experience.
Then your life will be beautiful, peaceful and rich."
—Peter Rosen

Money Is a Fruit of Your Thoughts

A truly wealthy person neither collects nor hoards. Money does not bring self-worth, it is one of the fruits of your thoughts.

Peter says, "Discover this great universal truth: Dreams come true as well as nightmares, because thought is the weaver of destiny." When your thoughts are right, whatever you do succeeds. There will be difficulties, but you know you can accomplish anything.

It's impossible to fail at what you set forth to do because it is in God's hands, and your hands are the only hands God has to use. God's divine energy pulses through you.

Success = Preparation + Opportunity

For an Olympic athlete, the journey is intense work and preparation. The last part is the triumph. This is delayed gratification.

Someone living a happy, successful, prosperous life is not lucky. He has prepared his thoughts and made life-affirming decisions for years. Plan your work and work your plan. Build your vision, work toward it, and your vision will manifest. When you are ready to give everything for your vision, achieving it is easier. Health, relationships and finances all improve when you are persistent with your plan.

Freedom is the ultimate form of success because you control your life. You cannot have any more freedom than you have control and you cannot have control without accepting responsibility for your life. When you are free you don't have to defend your beliefs, you don't have to explain and you don't have to complain. "Don't explain, don't complain, don't try and catch the wind."*

Negative people blame their misfortune on bad luck, karma, astrology or on others. If someone says, "I am unlucky," he blames others instead of taking responsibility for himself. Persistence is what most people call luck. Complainers never see the long hours of work that the successful person has endured. They do not realize that the so-called 'luck' they talk about is nothing more than long bouts of preparation meeting opportunity.

Don't think about luck. Risk more. Drill more wells. Remember the law of averages. If you want to get a coin to turn up heads 50 times, you'll need to flip it on the average of 100 times. Everything is probability. Do what works over and over, and you'll be successful at whatever you do.

Want More Money? Get a Job

Being of service equals prosperity. Give service and you will be prosperous. The universe always reciprocates. No one ever gets rich by cheating another person. They just get enough money to create a mess. If you want honest money, get a job. It is that simple. Just say, "I want a job. I want to work."

Poverty is a state of mind. Being broke can be temporary. People think if they try, they will fail. This builds up tremendous ego resistance to trying something new. The ego causes us to lose employment. When we think we are so incredibly important, we don't play the game the right way.

Vow to yourself to get honest. Think positively about solutions. Find your motivation. Trust the universe. Life can change in a pop.

Act Like Immigrants

Recognize what money you have. Base your assessment on reality. Then decide how much more you want and how to go about obtaining it.

Money is nothing more than a permission slip. How much permission do you want? You need to earn permission. You have to earn money and know you deserve it.

The Vietnamese came here believing everyone in America gets rich. So they did. Accustomed to hard work, they went to work. The average Korean family living here 20 years earns more than the average American because the immigrant believes in opportunities and hard work. At the turn of the century when the Irish, Germans, French and Scandinavians moved to America they all believed they could make their fortunes. Many did.

Anyone with fortitude and willingness to work for it can have all he wants. Thank God we can work and get paid for what we do. This is the land of milk and honey where everyone can get rich. Immigrants think this and it becomes true for them. See America through the eyes of an immigrant.

Improve Your Value of Service

If a 40-hour work week brings in just enough money to cover the basic necessities and you still want more, then work more or improve the value of your service. If you feel ashamed to ask for a fee, you have no self-worth. Ask for what you want.

This life is played by active participants, not by spectators sitting in the stands. When you live in the light of integrity, you work and prosper spiritually and financially.

Work is what we do when we would rather be doing something else. Turn work into play. Play with a shovel, a hammer or by investing money. Work smarter and more conscientiously and with love. Do your work knowing you cannot fail. Remember, money is an impartial tool. Improve your value of service, and others will give you money. When you excel in quality, your energy becomes wealth that grows and expands.

Like What You Do

External restoration can only occur when you restore your internal beauty and paradise. The key to restoring beauty is to offer excellence in whatever you do, whether stacking wood, digging ditches or teaching.

Liking what you do makes all the difference. This is a powerful spiritual law. Liking what you do leads to doing more of what you like. Make high performance your goal. Whatever you do, find it exhilarating. Want to do a good job.

Learn to deal with obstacles, such as difficult personalities in the office. Chip away at your ego. Meeting these challenges is also an accomplishment. Love obstacles in relationships because they build strength.

List Your Ten Favorite Things to Do

Choose an occupation you enjoy doing. If you don't know what career you want, list ten favorite things you enjoy doing enough to do without pay. List things you can pour your energy into that rejuvenate you, just as a hobby does. Make sure you do one of these for your career and livelihood.

Find a way to market what you do. The minute you make your first $1,000, you are a successful entrepreneur. You created your idea, worked for it and marketed it.

Commitment and investment bring out your best. It is exhilarating to be in business for yourself or a great company you invest in. If you don't own it, buy stock in it.

When we go to work *for* the company, not *in* it, we want to watch its value increase. Our personal commitment to it brings out the best in us.

Pay Yourself First

The first bill you must pay from your net income is 10% to yourself. You'll never miss it. Pay this bill the rest of your life. After you have paid yourself this 10%, budget your money and pay out the rest.

Put the 10% in an investment fund, or better yet, buy pure gold. Do not use this seed money for anything other than investments. That 10% will earn compound interest and will multiply like rabbits.

You can multiply that 10% in many ways. John D. Rockefeller worked for $3.80 a week. He gave $1.80 a week as seed money to people by giving a silver dime to everyone he met who was worthy of his gift. He knew what he gave away would come back ten times.

While you earn, carefully give small portions away. Seed money must be given wisely, especially to help someone start a business. The more you give away, the more returns to you.

Let compound interest multiply your seed money in a miraculous way. When you can, take 20% or more and invest it safely. The psychological power of investment is tremendous. Investments give you freedom. As soon as your investments make as much for you as your job, you can quit your job and travel. Give your extra money to friends or to save the rain forests. The money will continue to work for you.

Pay Your Bills Fast

Pay your bills right away. Put them in the mail, so they will not rob you of energy. A bill is a request to honor your word. Never see a bill as an enemy. This creates problems with bills. If you don't pay your bills, you defeat yourself and slander your promises.

If you want to do something on the spiritual path, it will happen when your financial house is in order. The universe is looking for people it can work with. It should not have to tell us to pay our bills or to make our word our honor. Our word and promise is important. If we are not sensitive to the basic things, then we can't experience the luminous life.

Beware of Addiction to Money

When you are ashamed of money or afraid you don't have enough, you are addicted to money. It is simply a medium of exchange. Locking it up takes it out of the marketplace, where it can work for you. When you say, "Go forth and multiply," your money will do just that.

The slightest addiction to money keeps it from growing. Your anxiety about holding on to it sends it running away as fast as it can. Don't dig it out to see what is happening all the time. Don't lock money up or it will escape. Do the opposite of what most people do. Give money freedom to go in the right direction and do not insulate it. Open your hands and heart and have no fear of losing what really doesn't belong to you permanently anyway. It will come back to you.

We become wealthy step by step. One of the steps is to just have fun giving money away. The divine cannot lose your money. If you want financial prosperity, give it away, and the divine will flood you with more. Donate to worthy causes that your heart feels good about.

We need to receive money to multiply it. Money is only a seed. When you receive seed money, some seeds may not grow and some may even die, but the crop will be abundant when you walk in the light. Re-invest and let it multiply.

Andrew Carnegie came to Pennsylvania as a Scottish immigrant and became the world's first billionaire. Do you think people who worked for him resented him? Forty-three of his employees became millionaires. He shared his wealth. He looked for the gold in people, then brought out the richness in them.

Philanthropic individuals make a difference in the world. They have given us lovely parks, libraries and museums. Only people who have power can get something done, and money is one form of power.

Wealthy people value quality products and service. If service and food are exceptional in a restaurant give a 25-30% tip, or 20% if it is good. You always get back what you give.

Create Quality

Greed destroys beauty by choking it. Greed pollutes the world. Peter says, "The solution to pollution is quality." You never see a trashed Rolls Royce in the junk yard. Buy quality and don't pollute. Items of quality last forever. Man's search for the fastest and cheapest has given birth to a greed that could destroy quality forever.

We need to experience quality people and things around us. Peter Douno, the Bulgarian Master, had a violin of such quality that the pure tone it produced repelled dissonant vibrations. He could clear out the rebels around him when he played it.

What quality do you create? How are you living a non-greedy, quality life? Make things that last forever. The quality of our Being determines the quality of our work, and the quality of our creation builds the quality of our Being.

Don't spend your life looking for bargains. Get things that last forever. Not buying quality results from a thought of lack. Who told you that you can't have the best? If people would raise their personal standards for excellence in the products they buy and the goods they consume, they would raise the level of competition of manufactured products so that only the longest lasting, non-polluting products would be purchased. There are no bargains on the counter of success. You happily pay full price if you're rich in spirit.

We live in a land of affluence and opportunity. We can find quality ways to live. Don't spend your life being a servant when you can live like a king. When you create beauty, your life feels good to you. Then you're in balance and the tension level is right.

God is in our excellent performance. What we hold inside cannot be hoarded. Express your inner talents and beauty. People who create beauty and quality in their lives know they cannot fail. Though they may be tested with challenges, they attract positive people and prosperity into their lives.

Free Yourself from Greed

Window shopping without any money in your pocket doesn't feel good. What you can't have often becomes irresistible. Let's suppose you go window shopping with money and you can buy anything you see. Do you have the same feeling of anxiety?

Now you don't want what you see, because there is no tugging or addiction. You only choose what is necessary for a comfortable lifestyle. Wealth can free us from addiction.

How do you get that feeling of freedom? Have enough money to cover your basics and play with the rest. Start with $1,000 in mad money, or if that is not possible, start with $100. Always have it with you. It gives you a feeling of self-esteem and freedom. You begin to say, "I could have this or I could have that, but I really don't want it right now." You have less urge to buy impulsively. Get used to the feeling of knowing you can buy what you want. A credit card will not work, because credit card companies bet on us overspending. Credit cards mean "I am indebted. I owe. I am enslaved."

If you do spend the money, immediately replace it and use it only for your own pleasure. Do this and you will feel rich. The $100 or $1,000 in your pocket gives you a wonderful sense of being wealthy, and you draw to yourself what you feel.

America's Founding Fathers Believed in Gold

Thoughts create prosperity, and our thoughts are rooted in our history. The Founding Fathers, though imperfect, held noble ideals. They loved liberty, light and happiness. The Constitution they created implied that if there are no victims there are no crimes. These Founders of the United States were people who dealt in value.

The Constitution said that no state would coin anything but gold and silver. This part of the Constitution has never been amended or taken out. Gold was used as money until President Franklin Roosevelt banned it from private ownership. Today it is again legal to own gold.

The early founders knew that one must build on the honest. Divine, universal laws were meant to be the foundation of our nation, and were intended for Washington D.C. It was designed and built on high spiritual values but has become corrupt. The "money changers" must be driven from the temple. If one builds under deception and fraud, success cannot last for long. When a country ceases to believe in honesty, it faces a debt it cannot pay.

The 1997 federal debt of the United States was estimated to be five and one half trillion dollars. It is not easy to grasp the magnitude of such a sum. A trillion dollars in one-hundred dollar bills laid end to end would circle the earth one hundred and forty-four times. If Columbus had borrowed ten thousand dollars every minute since 1492, the accumulated total would just now approach the one trillion dollar mark.

The United States keeps printing money, devaluing our dollars and decreasing our holdings. A financial crisis is inevitable. A key solution to the United States' economic dilemma is to return to the gold standard. Hold a certain amount of your wealth in gold. You will need it for financial survival.

Gold Is of Ultimate Value

The allure of gold is more than the metal. Legend has it that gold is solidified sunlight. Gold once was believed to be sunlight in the earth's crust. Some believe gold has physical and spiritual healing properties. All spiritual temples had gold in them.

The Sages of old would put a lump of gold at the base of grapevines so the root system would have light from below ground as the vines do from the heavens.

Gold is said to represent morality as well. Through time it has proven to be a trustworthy medium of exchange, and the color gold is a symbol of honesty and trust. All the gold ever mined and existing in vaults and in secret hiding places throughout the world remains of solid value. It is rare. All the gold ever mined in the world could be stacked on a basketball court. It can't corrode or rot. You can't print it. It cannot be counterfeited.

Gold and silver are portable commodities. A gold or silver coin has value anywhere.

Take Back Your Authority

People must be vocal about the gold standard before it can return. The issue must be put before the people for a vote. Enforcing the Constitution is essential to taking back our authority.

We must prepare to stand on Concord Bridge or in Lexington all over again. Love, passion and reason must prevail. Which high ideals will we defend? It is a spiritual quest. The days ahead will be neither easy, nor boring.

Here are some things you can do now:

- Get your own finances on solid ground.
- Hold no debt except hard property like real estate.
- Hold gold and silver.
- Be prepared and plan.
- Educate yourself and develop marketable skills.
- Be receptive to opportunities.
- An overcoming veil of light directs you.
- Right circumstances will appear.
- Remember, you are not alone.
- A higher order is appearing right on time.
- In a showdown between light and dark, light wins.

Wealth Is Energy

Spirituality is an abundance of energy. When we say a horse is spirited, we mean it has lots of energy. Energy enables us to accomplish things. The more we focus energy into an endeavor, the greater the results.

Hang-ups about wealth usually result from guilt or greed. Money is an extension of your self-esteem. What we say about ourselves is very important. Listen to what you think and say. You will lose everything if you are afraid of not having enough. Fear will make it so.

Your mind is your field. Plant what you want! Think it and you've got it. It's so simple. Focus on what makes your life comfortable. Expand your energy in those directions. You will get a return on your energy investment. The longer you work it, the more compound interest you'll have. This compound interest can be developed talents, accomplishments, training or financial success.

Wealth creators have learned the secret of multiplying their energy. Dale Carnegie created a mastermind group where their complete focus, empowered by zeal, created their wealth. The book, *Think and Grow Rich* by Napoleon Hill suggests more ways to create wealth.

Have Both Money and Time

Truly wealthy people have both money and time. They enjoy a sense of fullness. They do what they want, when and with whom they choose. We can be wealthy working at a gas station. We don't need a position or suit and tie. Use money wisely and for what you enjoy. Whatever you do that gives you pleasure and a sense of personal achievement is right for you.

"A truly wealthy person celebrates wealth in others. If we resent other people's success, we lock ourselves out of our own prosperity. The truly rich open the doors of their heart as easily as pushing a button for the elevator. Their hearts will take you as high as you're willing to go."*

Set Your Target and Fire Away

We can expect success if we set a target and aim at it persistently. Release your tension, and in a relaxed manner, shoot for the target with your intention. Focusing this mode of power strengthens you. You do not need to struggle. See, feel and know, just like a dancer, when you do the right thing. Investment in yourself works for you without effort. You can do nothing wrong. There is perfection in action.

Chart Your Goals and Progress

Writing your goals on paper is magic. Determine how much money you want to make this year and break it down into twelve month sections. Then, make a chart showing your income goal for each month. Put it up in the corner where you can see it. Record how much you bring in each month, and how close you are to your annual goal.

You build the nest egg step by step, not in big chunks of a hundred thousand a year, because your mind cannot accept having it that soon. A great mind set allows you to work on that piece of paper. Set your goal at the level that makes you stretch. Set it for less and you won't strive; for more and it's too much. You want just enough tension or stress. Distress deteriorates health, but some stress serves as healthy motivation.

One Good Idea

Once you have your chart, sit quietly in the morning (a great time to focus inwardly) and write ideas about how you can improve your productivity. How can you be better at what you do? Brainstorm new ideas with yourself. All you need is one great idea. Explore ways to improve, and one day you will get a brilliant idea.

Brad Walker was so stricken with multiple sclerosis that his body had nearly turned to stone. He wanted something to do with his life. He loved tropical fish, so he came up with an idea. He persistently contacted General Electric, and they made a special device to enable him to write with his tongue. He wrote several books about those fish, then learned to photograph them.

Brad Walker began making $40,000 a year doing what he loved. He grew beyond his limitations, and earned his sense of accomplishment. What gave him the power was just one good idea. There is nothing more powerful than an idea that comes into its own time.

Most of the Reward Comes Later

When you plant a certain Chinese bamboo tree, you water it and cultivate it for four years and nothing visible happens. The fifth year for the first six months you water and cultivate it and still nothing appears to happen. But in the final six months it grows 90 feet. The bamboo tree builds power in its seed form, and at the right time, bursts forth.

Like the Chinese bamboo tree, our visions and investments compound over time. Only after you apply your valuable time will you overcome obstacles. Focus on your target with relaxed confidence. Visualize, emotionalize and put it on paper. It will work if you do.

Chapter 6

Friendship

"If you love yourself and see your own value,
only then are you capable of seeing value in another."
—Peter Rosen

Give Love a Chance to Flower

Your first and foremost responsibility is to love your-self. Only then can you love others. When Jesus said, "Love your neighbor as yourself," he meant, love yourself first, then you can love another. Give love a chance to flower by being independently happy.

Who do you like to be around? Describe them. Are you so warm, happy and gentle that others love being around you? Do not burden your relation-ships with stiff rules of who must do what.

You must relate to yourself first with your head and heart before you can relate to someone else. Have 98% of your relating be to yourself, then 98% of you can relate to others. Personal honesty is required.

In the final analysis, love is all we have. Love is a miracle you must allow in order for it to flow through you. You are an elixir of love. Give others a big dose of this beauty you have inside.

Friendship Is the Greatest Wealth

If you have one best friend or two or more loyal friends, your Kingdom is vast and your wealth beyond measure. Give away friendship and you will always have enough. People are lonely for a friend. Peter says, "To have a friend, you must be a friend, first." We light the fires one heart at a time with friendship.

A friend covers over the faults of another. He exalts his friend's virtue, talent and abilities. He supports his endeavors. Do your friendships demonstrate loyalty? Only a loyal friend is worthy of your honor. Only a loyal friend enriches your life. Be around people who have learned true peace. Gently release those whose word is not their honor.

Our Words Soothe or Destroy

Every word that comes from your mouth has color, music and scent, and creates energy in the air. You hear more than physical speech; its invisible vibration massages or maims. You communicate through vibrations of words, harmoniously or not.

Speaking or thinking words with great energy powerfully creates rapid results. Be aware of what you hold in your mind. The words you have in your heart and mind are powerful. Angry people create a smell. Loving people perfume the air. Anger and hurt tear up and depress the cells. Love and laughter heal them.

Let the words of your mouth and the meditation of your heart enhance your world. Deal with people lovingly. Stop the negative words before they come out of your mouth. Bite your lip if you have to. Learn not to speak critically, and then not to even think critically. It is not our job to correct people, but to accept them as much as possible.

Do not gossip. The heart hurts when you gossip and start being picky. Be aware of any slander in your daily life. When you indulge in gossip or vicious criticism of others your body will age as fast as those of mudslinging politicians during election time. It is absolutely impossible for anyone to bombard his environment with negative expressions and remain healthy. Do not discourage the spirit of another. Replace negativity with positive love.

Mean What You Say

Most people don't pay any attention to what they say and then wonder why they have difficulties. People who say, "Life is so miserable" kill themselves in one way or another. They speak unconsciously. Examine the sounds they make when they speak, and you will see something very profound concerning the quality of their lives.

Be attentive to the words you speak and the tone you use. You create either beauty or limitation with your thoughts and words. By developing the beautiful, whether a body, talent or way of performing, you bring excellence into the world. Do not whine and say, "I'm not good at anything" or "I can't." If you make these statements, the universe grants them.

If you don't trust yourself, you won't trust others. If you don't trust others, you program them to disappoint you. Never say others are untrustworthy.

They may act out your powerful statements of distrust. Be ever so thoughtful about how your words program yourself and others.

Your words must be honest and true. When you give your word, you make a statement to your Being that is your bond of honor. An unpunctual person is a liar in many things. Peter says, "If you're not early, you're late; if you're late, you're a liar." If your words have no meaning, then your promises are lies.

When we stay true to our word, we are blessed and free. When we speak truth, we feel a rush inside us. Truth gives birth to light.

You use words as tools to construct your emotional state and your environment. If your words do not say exactly what you want them to say, you will have a haphazard life. Clearly saying what you mean strengthens the fabric of your aura. You gain confidence when you speak with honesty and integrity. You turn your stumbling blocks into stepping stones.

Speak less. Say only what benefits yourself and others. Then be quiet. Don't say, "but...but...but..." You're done. Say no more.

Practice this, so when you speak your words have power. Pauses are necessary. You say more by saying less. Sometimes not saying says it all.

Privacy

Tell someone all about your life and you give them ammunition as critics. If you like what the critics give you, good. If you don't like what you hear, so be it. That is also okay. Keep some parts of your life private. What matters is who you are now.

Talking About Your Goals

Never discuss your goals with someone who doesn't support them. Choose carefully any person or persons you take into your confidence. They must be completely supportive. In most instances it is better to tell no one. Let it percolate within yourself.

Focus and silence accomplish great things. At times, choose to be in silence with your ideas. Silence increases your idea's energy as powerfully as a pressure cooker. It takes integrity to hold on to a secret.

Then, when you do express your goals, the sound vibrations of your words go into the ether and manifest your ideas as a decree of the Divine. Focused silence followed by carefully stated goals creates like a magic wand. When you describe something with power in your words, the universe energizes it. Your thoughts obey you, and every spirit being comes to your service to help you hit your targets. These little angels bring back to you what you decree.

You have no power to ask, if you have no power in your words. Thoughts create words, words create emotions, and emotions create the power to materialize.

A second school of thought on sharing goals with others is the audible proclamation. The person saying, "This shall be" has no way out. The difficulty is that many people will question it and say, "Oh, sure." This challenge stifles your energy to accomplish what you want.

When you are self-aware, you subject yourself to no one. You are unaffected by others' opinions. Your auric field radiates outwardly, and you create whatever you target with your mind. When you call on the universe, it will give you the courage to use those rare words, "Yes, I can do it. I can and I will. I can, I will and I am." These words lead boldly to success. To do anything, first you must believe you can do it.

It is time the whole world slows down. But you must slow down first. Everyone is rushing about and needs to slow down. When you rush, life becomes a roller coaster ride of dizzying heights and nauseating lows. Take some time to become real. Read the *Velveteen Rabbit*. Read it again. Once you become real you can never become unreal again. Realness lasts an eternity, but it takes a whole lifetime to become real.

Too often we are busy, and as we rush, we snap at people we love. We get so hurried that we have to say to ourselves, "Slow down, peace, be still."

Excuse Me, I'm Getting Ready to Hang Up

When talking with friends do not use them as garbage dumps. Don't tell your problems, only your victories. Refuse to listen to rudeness. If people treat you like a garbage dump, say, "Excuse me, I'm getting ready to hang up." Only those with low self-esteem can think of themselves as garbage dumps, ready to accept others' trash.

Explore problems constructively. Make certain the focus is on the solution, not the problem. Do not wallow in the problem and do not rehash it over and over. Here is a five-step process for solving problems:

1. Ask, "What is the worst that could happen?"
2. Accept it.
3. Evaluate options for bettering the situation.
4. Choose one of them.
5. Take action immediately.

If life-promoting results occur, you've chosen correctly. If not, go back to step two.

Love Is All We Have

There is no love without freedom, and no freedom without love. If two people both feel romance, it's fine. But, if two people are needy, you have trouble. You cannot be demanding in relationships. You can only earn love. A freebie doesn't work. Be loved for your value, not for your begging. A weak person blames a stronger person if he falls down.

Perform with excellence as you relate to the person you live with. Let your "I Am" be the highest of the high. Develop high self-esteem and treat others well. People feel good about themselves when they do a good job, and then they treat you well.

You can only be loving when you are proud and strong. Ask, "For what virtues am I loved?" and strengthen them. Be powerful within yourself, not over others.

Hold Your Own Power

What others say or do need not have power over you unless you give your power to them. We may adopt religions or become slaves or worshippers because we fear making mistakes. The herd mentality takes us to mediocrity. Who would really want to be just like the masses? It is difficult to get straight A's in life and make no mistakes. Be authentic and totally honest. Speak from your heart.

What is your personal self-talk? It's hard to stop self-talk that says you're angry, bad, sad or anxious. You are lord and goddess of the heavens and you have incredible power when you function with awareness. Remember, your word is your magic wand. Whatever you say about yourself comes true.

Living life with exuberance involves wins and losses, but you'll ultimately tip the scales in the most rewarding directions. Be yourself, with or without approval. You are free when you live on the edge with honesty, standing on your own two feet.

The rebel in you will give you the courage to live on the edge. The rebel is powerful and positive. When you decisively control the direction, the rebel frees you to choose your life circumstances.

Love = Defenselessness = Freedom

Freedom is not being defensive. Instead, believe you are your own proof, and have no need to defend your beliefs, opinions or lifestyle. Do not lock up your energy by taking offense, or you will suffocate in your cocoon. With love you take less offense at injury. If you are beyond taking offense, forgiveness never enters the situation, because there's no need to forgive unless you take offense.

When you realize that love equals freedom, you live the life you choose. To be all that you want to be, you must be free to disagree. Disagreement can be grand.

Anger Is Frustrated Energy

You get angry when you feel hurt and powerless to control yourself, others or circumstances. You can't control others or circumstances, but you can control your thoughts and their consequent emotions.

When you don't use angry energy constructively, it backs up and destroys you. Unconsciously expressed anger is a form of violence that attacks the self. People with a lot of held in anger, resentment, confusion and malice attract the development of cancer. Rebellious cancer cells oppose the natural, peaceful state of your body. Unconsciously expressed anger is a form of insanity unaware of how it affects yourself and others. If you are unconscious you react with flight or fight.

Love yourself enough to learn how to express anger constructively. Anger is only frustrated energy. Give your anger a constructive channel, such as physical exercise. When we consciously experience people, we are aware that their scent and vibration affect us, and we respond consciously. Peter says, "Anger is never proper, but its energy can be used constructively. Never create negative scenarios that are alive with emotion. This is the first responsibility of a rational being."

To be less reactive, develop your understanding. Look at what hurt or offended you before you felt the anger. Forgiveness heals hurt. Communicate your forgiveness and act accordingly. Then you'll free yourself of anger, be sane and produce sane results. An abundant heart and focused mind create peaceful behavior.

Feel Out of Place?

People with integrity don't attack their opponents. A person who does not know his self-worth has anger storms and attacks others. Have little or no association with negative people until you are strong enough to extend your own radiance and energy as a buffer to protect you.

Don't spend your time with people who are always having problems. Don't sit there and let them drain you. Handle their negativity by holding your light or leaving the room politely. Do this with anyone who starts to vomit their negativity on you. You are not a garbage dump. Excuse yourself until he is in a better mood.

If you feel out of place, get out of the place. If you are positive and working hard on yourself to get yourself clean, don't let people throw mud on you. Develop your problem solving skills and deepen your compassion for others without allowing them to dump more negativity on you than you can handle.

To Heal, Have an Open Heart

Friendship is loving with great empathy. The open heart requires you to speak as truthfully as possible. Speak out of love and be loving. Love is the only healer. You heal the world when you wish no one harm. Have compassion for others and be responsible for yourself. Vincent Lombardi said, "Fatigue makes cowards of us all." Be aware of the times you do things unlike the you that you want to be. Say, "That's not the performance I want." If what you do feels lousy afterwards, do it differently in the future.

Many people have to feel bad before they decide to live differently. Don't stop people from feeling the strong emotions necessary to see the reason for change. Do you have to feel the pain or can you change by listening to the whispers? The saying goes that if you don't listen to the whispers, you will have to hear the shouting, and if you don't listen to the shouting, you will have to hear the crashing. Some keep hitting their heads against the same cinder block wall. Be conscious and conscientious.

A Loving Person Has No Fear

We can become prisoners of other people's thoughts by fearing their condemnation of us. We often fear we cannot perform in certain ways. We have fears of not having enough or of not being in control. Fear gives birth to old problems, confusing our thoughts. We can choose our thoughts. We are all light. We must dispel the clouds that hide the sun within us.

One symbol of the heart is the lion. The Hebrew word for lion is "lev," which sounds like "love." When you radiate your lion-hearted love, fear is banished. When fear is cast aside true love shines. You cannot have love and fear or love and hate in the same package. You will be preoccupied with one or the other.

The Gnostic Gospel of Thomas written in Madras, India tells us to be like little children who can take their clothes off and trample them under their feet, dancing unashamedly, unabashedly, unconditionally in the light of the Kingdom of God. This is being in innocence.

In innocence, the Self is Divine because it is I-Am-ness. We are here to feel full ranges of emotions and then choose what we want. It is important to act from rational self-interest in terms of I-Am-ness. This is self care.

Life Is Like Peeling an Onion

Guilt gives birth to fear. When you feel guilty, you fear disapproval from God, parents, church, friends, politicians or your spouse. The fear of disapproval leads to compulsive compromise.

Peel away your basic fears like the layers of an onion's skin. With each layer the tears come, and you peel that layer away, too. Finally, you find the empty space where it all is. You are empty and full at the same time. When you have peeled the onion down, you end up with the invisible light striking all objects and consciousness beyond the veil of tears.

This empty space is within the atoms that make up the galaxies. It empowers you. Replace the immobilizing fear of making wrong choices and decisions with the knowledge that if you take a wrong turn on the highway, you may simply turn back and decide again. This is the real "high way" to do things.

If you doubt or despair, simply dust yourself off, stand tall, refocus your eyes on the prize and go on, go on, go on!

Your Conclusions Create Your Emotions

Feel good and want your friends to feel good. To heal your world you must be happy. Happy thoughts create happy emotions. Your emotions are the sum total of your past conclusions. You store judgments and evaluations in your mind that together form a picture that creates who you think you are. The thousands of similar events that you evaluate give birth to your dominant range of emotions.

To be radiantly happy, draw correct conclusions. Love truth more than approval. Embrace facts, not fear. Peel away every layer of lies and you will fly high in freedom, happiness and light.

Your Happiness Is My Highest Value

The quickest way to ruin a relationship is to impose rules and regulations. Laws are created out of fear by and for those who do not control themselves. The opposite of fear is love. Love says, "You are free to do anything you want to do. I trust that you will do what is thoughtful and kind." Over time, the proof is in the pudding.

When you are authentic, you have no emotional locks or chains to keep people out. Innocence means you are fresh. Live within a framework of love, not law. The Christ spirit has no limitations. It delivers a spiritual burst of energy. The Christ sets you free from all laws except to love one another and love the Divine with all your heart, strength, soul and mind.

A relationship will not work unless both individuals are emotionally independent. Two happy, independent people can have a fabulous relationship. They are complementary to each other.

Differences are just fine because whole hearts believe in liberty and the pursuit of happiness. Be quick to apologize if you make a mistake. Say to your companion, "I want you to please yourself first. Then you'll be happy, and that's my greatest happiness."

Be a Pillar

In a relationship, two individual pillars stand strong and tall. They do not lean on one another. Respect is the key. If you do not respect your friend, you begin to make demands of him. "Spect" means "to see." "Respect" means "to see twice." Look carefully, then look again. Conscientiously respect others. Look for qualities that you respect.

"If you love me, you would . . . " is a set-up. Doing something for someone else is a gift. You have no duty to others' expectations. They are not entitled to your gifts. To respect and honor others, develop your compassion.

Being a pillar also implies standing tall. Discern what is in your sphere of influence and what is not. You are not a fireman who must put out people's fires. You get into enough trouble starting them. Do not assume responsibility *for* others. Rather, learn to be responsible *to* others. This keeps you from becoming a rescuer and allows others to take responsibility for themselves.

We Teach Others How to Treat Us

What you allow or tolerate teaches others what is acceptable to you. Examine all your relationships:

- How do you treat others?
- What are they tolerating?
- How do others treat you?
- What are you allowing?
- There are no victims, only volunteers.

Seek the cause, not the effect. Rather than seek unearned love, take time to understand the causes of love. Earn love by being authentically loving and kind. These conditions must exist to receive love. Be more than the common crowd languishing in love-lessness. Rather than expect unconditional love, establish conditions that make you lovable. You don't get respect by being unrespectable.

Be the cause, instead of seeking the effect. See and treat others in harmony with your integrity. Treat others and teach others to treat you with thoughtful kindness.

Truth Is Simple, Lies Are Complex

Live honestly and you will live simply. When you see truthfully, you invest in making things work. Whatever you perceive and visualize is your truth, and it is a self-fulfilling prophecy.

The greatest lie is that we are powerless; the greatest truth is that we have miracle material within. The more we harmonize our lives with the light of truth, the more powerful we become.

When you perform authentically, you are free. Don't dance to someone else's music. Dancing to your own music is the expression of inward delight. The honesty of your decision creates your future.

Embrace the truth. Quit worrying about making a fool of yourself. Do not shake your head in agreement if you don't agree. You can only be yourself when you recognize that you are free.

Show Beauty When You Deal with People

What we do reveals our motives. Think of the Biblical Mary and Martha. They were so hospitable. They couldn't do enough for Jesus. Their activities reflected the pure motives of their hearts.

Show beauty through caring. You can feel plenty without choosing to suffer. Compassion never threatens your happiness and health, nor does it imply loss.

Life Is a Playground

The fruit of the spirit is love, joy and peace. When you play life and have fun, you multiply the joy and turn up the voltage.

You don't have to know or understand it all. The universe just asks you to watch on the inside. The Nazarene said to the Samaritan woman at the well, "The water that I will give will become a spring inside providing life-giving water and eternal life" (John 4:14).

Christ's energy can only grow in your heart. One of the most beautiful things you can have is a friend. Jesus extolled the virtues of friendship even to the point of referring to himself as the friend. Imagine this world being made up of only best friends playing in the playground of life.

Chapter 7

Healing

"What we truly desire we visualize and create,
be it the outcome of our hopes or our fears."
—Peter Rosen

Own Your Peace

Your first and foremost responsibility is to your own peace. That dynamic, magnetic energy either draws people to you or repels them. The more peaceful you are, the stronger your magnetism.

You cannot simultaneously hold negative thoughts or images and expect health. Whatever you give your attention to cannot go away, because you feed it with your faith in its coming true. Attention feeds a thought, and a thought becomes a thing. Beware if sickness gives you pay-offs such as attention from others. Attention prolongs disease.

Don't spend too much energy trying to find logical reasons for why you are sick instead of focusing on your health. This entrenches the illness further. If you are sick and talk about sickness, you get more of it.

All healing requires dissolving poison. To do this, focus on love, laughter, excitement and meaningful-ness. Focus always on what you want materially, physically, emotionally and spiritually, not on what you don't want. Be positive and embrace God's gift of peace. When you are negative, you decline the gift set before you. If it's a great day and you are neg-ative, you are refusing to partake in the beauty around you.

"I'm Getting Better"

Choose life by becoming increasingly definitive. You have the power within you to act on life. If you acted in a way that did not pay off in an affirming direction, choose again.

When you are sick, and you're asked how you feel, say, "I'm getting better." Whatever you affirm long enough will manifest.

All Illness Is Dis-Ease

Discomfort creates disease. If you feel uncomfortable, you have disease. If you feel comfortable, you are healthy. Never hold onto the investment of feeling uncomfortable. "How many darken their lives with heavy, earthquake-like thoughts? Every complaint, every thought of weakness, every thought of envy constricts the solar plexus and robs you of heart, or courage, thus bringing imbalance into your life."*

You choose how you feel. Anxiety is fear without an object, usually an imagined fear not proven logically. Anxieties give birth to physical illness. Dizziness may result from self-doubt about being able to maintain balance in life. Ulcers don't result from what you eat, but from what's eating you, from the things you can't digest about life. Ulcers are more about irritations.

Physical swelling and bruising is a protection. If a person feels emotionally bruised, the body retains fluids and puts on more fat. Frequently, people with water retention have been emotionally bruised. People who believe a hard time is coming put on weight to tide them over the lean times.

Physical pain relates to an emotional state. Whenever you have a physical ailment or health issue, don't turn it into guilt. Playfully and non-judgmentally explore the emotions connected to it. Seriousness stiffens the body. Watch your world with aliveness, not sleepiness.

Healing Crisis

Healing crises do have an important role. When you start doing good things and taking care of yourself, you release the toxins. You'll feel sick while these are coming out. After you cleanse yourself you have fewer and fewer healing crises.

The body will give you feedback. Listen to the body by listening to your thoughts. You never have an illness or an accident without being warned ahead of time.

Real wealth is within your spirit. You have so much life and power to heal yourself. You are an undiscovered galaxy. The power of spirit and being is your birthright. You are all that and more, for you are part of God. God is the life within you. Do not limit God or yourself. Author and thinker Florence Scovel Shinn said, "I will not limit God by finding limitation in myself."

What Are You Afraid Of?

What you fear you suffer over. All suffering is mental, whereas pain is a fact or sensation. When you add suffering to pain you have agony. Suffering is a big deal because you make it that way.

Pain will always heal, though it may take a long time. It heals more quickly when you renounce suffering based on your fears and expectations. You cannot suffer unless you project your fear by way of a negative expectation. If you eliminate the expectation, fear dies, eliminating the cause of suffering. Negative expectation is a future projection: You're afraid . . . you project . . . you suffer. Stop projecting and you stop suffering. When you renounce your fears, suffering and pain, you are free.

Fear and suffering come from holding on to negative thoughts. Fears are magnets that draw more fear to us. Encounter your fears. Only then will you know they are illusions.

You Have Control

If you want to be healed, you are. If you don't want to be and your belief system doesn't allow it, you will not be. Watch closely what you think. You have to believe, "I am responsible for this ailment and I have control over it."

The tissue in the stomach is replaced every few minutes. Your skin regenerates itself and totally changes within 30 days. The skeleton constantly changes. But do you let your thoughts change and rejuvenate also? Bernie Segal notes in his book, *Love, Medicine and Miracles*, that one of his patients said, "Being sick is what I do the best." Stop negative habit patterns or they will repeat and repeat and repeat.

The body can be kept young a lot longer than 100 years. It is designed to be around. To stay young you must constantly regenerate your thoughts, views and beliefs, or they create clouds in the auric field. The auric field is like an electromagnetic cloud surrounding the physical body. Positively charged ions stick to us like carbonized clouds in the aura.

To take the dense clouds out of the auric field so the body can heal, say, "This moment is God in perfection." These present moments continue and become our eternity. When we are free, our physical and emotional selves heal simultaneously. We are free when we know that nothing dies. Death is the most deceptive myth. It creates judgments that make us feel unworthy.

Pay attention to your dreams, but understand they often simply release excessive mental refuse. Dreams fueled by strong aspirations are countless concentrated thoughts coming together to produce your intense goals or visions. When you're passionate about your aspirational dreams, you produce endorphins that empower you tremendously.

Miracles occur when you give health laser-like focus. Know exactly what you want to do. Is there an area in your life you have been holding back from the emphatic "Yes, I can do it?" If so, take heart, take courage and start now.

No Accidents

There are no accidents. The universe works from an infallible law of cause and effect. We are the final authority responsible for our lives. Health issues may be more than they appear to be. For example, someone may hurt his knee because he held his back stiffly. At a largely unconscious emotional and psychological level, guilt and self-doubt may contribute to the injury. If life has been painful, a person may bring his shoulders forward to protect the heart area.

Carrying heavy emotional loads may complicate chronic back or knee problems.

If someone has been defensive for a long time, he may lock his arms over his chest because it hurts to feel. A tender heart needs protection. His arms may even close over the solar plexus. You get a "gut reaction" from the solar plexus because of the electricity there. The solar plexus feels.

Smiles and Laughter Heal

When you feel good about yourself, you radiate high energy. When you smile at others, you calm their fears and help reduce their negative emotions. Smiling allows your light to radiate from your eyes. When you smile that energy comes back to you. Everyone has light. This beautiful energy protects you from negative energy and heals you by attracting positive energy from others who also feel good about themselves.

This is a sacred and healing secret: Develop humor and awareness. Deal with your fears. Some of them don't have anything to do with this lifetime, but result from potent learning experiences of previous lives. With humor and awareness, you can develop your abilities, and when you have exhausted them, other unseen helpers will be there.

Happy people live in a happy world. They know life is a 24 hour meditation.

Call Rotten Things Rotten

If you have feelings of abandonment, just drop them. Look at where your thoughts are. Be aware. Don't go to the old dead past and dig up the bones. Be pure, so you can receive with an open door and an uncluttered mind. Name the feelings, then let them go.

Despite all the rotten things, the divine drama is pretty neat. Life doesn't have to be taken so seriously. The first time that you can leave your body and return, you know there is no death. With that awareness you appreciate life with gratitude.

Sometime between 412 and 323 B.C., an unusual man named Diogenes lived in Athens, Greece. Diogenes was totally empowered, confident and at peace. He appreciated authenticity and spent his whole life looking for authentic people who were free to be themselves. He even carried a lantern with him that he would shine in people's faces, even in broad daylight. When asked what he was doing he would say, "Trying to see if you are authentic or not."

A powerful person is like Diogenes, unashamed of showing sensitivity or strength. High self-esteem comes when you value what is inside you.

Drop all nonsensical pastimes. You don't have to go back and unravel things. Don't argue, whine or compete. What is done is done. An awakened person lets trivial things simply roll off his back. Accept your grace. Be at ease, not full of dis-ease.

Love Is in Your Hands

God has put in your hands the power to heal yourself and others. The energy of love is the healing element, and claiming the light sets us free from the past. You have the power to start the healing process when you say, "I can, I will and I am!"

Injuries heal when you believe they can and tell them to heal. Bones can get hot and go back into place. A person who can run energy will find his hands very warm while assisting the healing. Some can see the heat energy emanate from a healer's fingers.

You have not been taught that you have the power to heal. Suspend your disbelief. To heal, say, "I know this works," and just do it. A mother does this unconsciously with every embrace of her crying, hurt child. When you believe there is nothing wrong with you, there is nothing wrong. Our minds drive our bodies, not the other way around. Your body has a healthy image or mold of itself and will right itself if you believe it can and give it permission. When you celebrate yourself and your health, you celebrate God. Trust your own judgment, not what others say. Trust your feeling of rightness. The answers always exist inside. Your immune system speaks to you through definite feelings. Chemicals become feelings. You will have an inner knowing that you are healing, or that you are dying. There is abundant scientific evidence that a person can postpone dying until a certain date, like Christmas, a birthdate or a visit from a son who must travel thousands of miles to get there. You have the final say with your body.

Watch Your Wishes

There is a story of a man sitting under a tree who was given the gift of his thoughts instantly becoming reality. First, he said, "I am hungry." Poof! There was food. Then, he thought, "I am thirsty." Poof! He had something to drink. Next, he thought, "This is too good to be true. There must be a demon playing a trick on me." Poof! There was a demon. Then he thought, "Maybe it will eat me." Poof! He was gone.

A double-blind experiment was conducted at the University of Texas on patients with cancer. All were told that one half of the group had a placebo and one half were being treated with a new type of chemotherapy. None were told which they received.

Three percent of the people with the placebo lost their hair as if they were on chemotherapy. The mind is that powerful. The body obeys our thoughts and wishes.

All illness starts with a thought form. Your thoughts give birth to emotions, and the chemical result of an emotion is a neuropeptide. Cancer is an illusionary thought held in some rebellious cells that can override your thoughts. You can say to those illusionary thoughts, "Hey, out the door."

The individual with AIDS visualizes the consequences he has seen, and these visualizations create emotions. A person with AIDS has seen so much death and destruction that his thoughts, visualizations and emotions bear the fruit of his thoughts. We choose power or weakness, blessings or maledictions.

Don't Live in Your Own Excrement

A sensitive person can walk into a room full of bad vibrational energy and pick up on the sticky, unclean, excremental thoughts. Some people live in the stench of a slum unconscious of the pollution they live in. A low vibrational astral-level consciousness creates the problems resulting in disturbed homeless people, alcoholics and drug addicts. Their vibrations draw these psychic experiences.

Physical sickness lives in the ethers first. The first sign of holding negative thoughts is revealed in your posture changes. You start looking and bending downward. Your face tells when you've been holding heavy expressions.

Self-talk like "I am happy" goes from the top of the head to the tip of the toes. Negative self-image comes from negative self-talk. Negative thinking is the same as having a butter body that has turned rancid. Negativity makes the body arthritic.

A courageous person always associates with Luminous Beings and thoughts. As you have fewer negative thoughts, your being pulls toward the Light. You hold your entire body posture straighter and higher and are drawn to the Sun. The Sun is a luminous thought. You are an electric resonator either giving off healthy or unhealthy vibrations at any given time. Good thoughts give off healing waves.

Feel Good About Yourself

Illness and pain are tender and touchy issues. To heal, love yourself deeply and in an awesome fashion. Create a scene of beauty as the background of any difficulty you might be experiencing. It will ease the challenge and soften it into healing.

While conducting an experiment on immunity levels, a doctor at Harvard University had people watch movies of Mother Theresa taking care of the poor. After viewers watched this video, their immunity increased. The same audience was then shown a video depicting the horrors of war. Their immunity decreased.

Miracles occur when we act from nurturing love. Plants and animals grow and people heal. God is love and where there is love, there is healing. We are a part of God. Love does the work.

When you feel good about yourself, you know the heart is king. The heart is not an emotion; it is an energy vibrating in waves around you. Just love people and they will heal. Great things are done in secret.

It Hurts to Hold On All the Time

When you get addicted to your clothing (the body), you experience trouble and pain. Scar tissues disappear if you don't hold on to the old scars emotionally and physically. Scar tissues are only memories.

It hurts to hold on all the time. When you relax, you are gently lifted up. When you are happy and feel good about yourself, self-esteem soars to the sky. You feel, walk and smile like all is right and light in the world you create. A light-hearted being flies high in the open sky. Be light and lifted up.

Love Is Vibrational Magic

Throw guilt out the window and be responsible for yourself. Do not criticize harshly even your own performance. If you perform poorly simply say, "That's not like me. I'll do better next time." When you direct your destiny you live as an example, and your energy, connected vibrationally to others, affects them. All you need to do is put yourself together, and your vibration will emanate. When you are whole you will heal others magically when you think of them. Before long the whole world will be whole.

How? Love is the vibrational magic. The electrical field of your aura influences people even before you speak. The radiance of your energy field will heal difficulties in the body that result from confused, negative thinking. When you feel wonderful you will heal yourself. Be in the center, be still — not too tight or too loose.

Buddha noticed a young disciple so intent on attaining enlightenment that he gave up the most precious thing he loved, his music, and went into the forest barefoot and without protection. It was easy for Buddha to find the young man by following the blood his feet left on the jagged gravel. Along the way Buddha picked up the young man's stringed instrument. He found the young man far back in the jungle attempting to meditate.

Buddha sat there, not saying a word, trying to tune the instrument. He plucked on it, but the strings were too loose, so nothing came out. At last the young man said, "You've got to tighten the string. It's not in tune." So Buddha started tightening and tightening and the young man yelled, "No, no, no, no, they're too tight. Let me have that." He took the instrument and began adjusting the strings. He said, "It's got to be not too tight and not too loose." And Buddha said, "Yes, just like you. Not too tight, not too loose."

Don't be extreme. Just watch for the center. Float and the river will take you home.

Thymus and Immune System

Thoughts create emotions which produce neuropeptides. Thoughts allow the thymus gland to expand or shrink. Your thymus directs your immune system. Smiling focuses and directs a tension that stimulates the brain to create endorphins, a natural opiate that allows the thymus gland to create healing T cells, B cells, macrophages, lymphocytes and interferon. Pleasant emotions and thoughts result in happiness and health.

Under stress and conflict the thymus gland can shrink to one-half its size. Stress comes when you lack a plan of action or cannot see your options. You cannot have stress if you're constructively doing something to arrive at a solution. Positive or right action stimulates the thymus gland.

Every thought has a chemical reaction in the pituitary gland that directs the thymus to send out healing biochemical messages. This thought-to-immune system is a two-way road. When the white blood cells of your immune system produce the virus fighter interferon, your thoughts become more assertive. When the immune system is charged up, you feel powerful about your life. Health follows.

Even the AIDS virus is influenced by thoughts. The structure of the AIDS virus is almost identical to that of neuropeptides, the chemical equation of thought and emotion. This suggests that like the virus, thought and emotion have great power to create.

Have you ever felt ill when you have been ecstatically happy? I doubt it. AIDS sufferers and those with immune deficiency must feel good about themselves by loving who they are and letting go of guilt. There is no problem without a solution. Focus on the solution.

Smiles, laughter and meaningful thoughts all stimulate the thymus gland to be strong and healthy. Smiles and laughter heal. You simply cannot be sick when you are happy. But given 24 hours of extreme distress or conflict, watch out!

With high self-esteem you will be healthier. Do not replay old self-doubt tapes that lead to illness. Be decisive and have direction, even if it is wrong. You can always change directions later.

Remember, if you're not getting what you want, change what you think and do. Ask your heart in the silence, and listen for its answer. The more in touch you are, the more power you have.

Sinus Cavities and Psychic Energy

The five sinus cavities resonate as psychic energy centers when kept free of mucus. A pure diet, clean air and good exercise will open the sinus cavities. Here are a few other tools to help clear sinuses.

Goldenseal taken as a tea or in capsules can reduce mucus and ease breathing. Oils like Hi Chi Oil rubbed on the sinus externally can help, too. Vitamin C also helps clear the sinus. Drop the milk and dairy products. Keeping the sinuses clear and clean enhances psychic ability.

You'll retain fluids if you think things are slipping through your grasp. When you hold onto life you clutch up and hold yourself tight. Constipation also results from holding on. Be aware of your body language expression of holding on and allow yourself to release. Do not wear tight things around your neck or waist.

Healing Scents and Sounds

The energy forms of music and incense can counteract the negative. Incense was originally used to create a mood and to drive out negative thoughts. Use incense or real flowers in your home to enhance its positive energy. Myrrh is a scent that represents love. Frankincense represents peace.

When you mean what you say, the body will obey. You control your body's aging and health. Say, "I can, I will and I am." "I am proud that I did that" is a sound statement that recognizes your power. Jesus used sounds to heal. He walked through the crowds and said, "You are healed."

Think about the music you listen to. It affects your cellular structure and can sicken or heal you. Music creates geometric designs. Some music creates the healing energy design of the pentagram. You are like a pentagram, you have two arms, two legs and a head. This pentagram shines like the Bethlehem star in all of us.

Be fed by music and its vibrations. Be especially aware of music during a meal. As you refine this energy, you gain nourishment from the tones themselves. Musical tones can make statements that lift the human spirit to divine levels. Calm and energizing music feeds the light or electromagnetic body. The musical note C resonates with the color vibration of red. Going an octave higher brings in more light, a more pastel color. All sounds are colorful.

The correct use of sounds is essential to our well-being. In the Old Testament, the walls of Jericho crumbled when the trumpets blew and the people gave a great shout. There are accounts of Tibetans using tone vibrations to lift ten-ton stone slabs up mountains. Hitler's scientists built a cannon to shoot sound vibrations that would shatter stone walls, but as it was perfected, the individuals creating it fell ill.

A Melody of Music in the Spheres

What you perceive and think has a vibrational effect on your life. If you are sensitive to vibrations, the beautiful will often move you to tears of gratitude. When you cultivate awareness, appreciation and gratitude, you create a new song in the music of the spheres that is carried through the realms of heaven. Your thoughts create the melody.

When in resonance, you and whatever or whomever you're with vibrate together. You are a vibrational entity who communicates what you feel. As you broadcast your thoughts, you emit electromagnetic frequencies that either harmonize or disrupt the cells in that electromagnetic field. When discordant thoughts prevail, discord destroys the cellular structure of your body. When harmonious thoughts prevail, that harmony enlivens and charges every cell of your body.

Your Mantra Is Within You

Certain mantras have healing powers so profound and dynamic that specific sound combinations are held in highest secrecy. You will discover the mantra for you when you demonstrate that you are responsible for it. You are not dependent on anyone for it. You have it within.

Chanting the "Om" or "I Am" produces circles of healing energy. The circle's resonance equates to that of light, which represents all. The astrological symbol for sun, a dot in a circle, signifies the infinite, the eternal, the light. "Om" creates and draws the light. The sound of the "Om" is the vibrational energy behind the sun.

Experience Your Heart

The universe gives you the opportunity to experience your heart as you give to life. Giving is life. Holding on is death. To be truly vibrant, let life flow through you. You have gifts to give. What are your gifts? How are you giving them?

Do what you do with excellence, and you give the highest you have. Others will experience your heart energy through your giving. Hold faith in your beauty. Have the courage to live that faith in action.

Choose Ye This Day to Live

Life and death are your choice. When you choose life, every day is a new beginning, fresh and alive. Your intentions and commitments determine the day's quality. When you have purpose, your physical body lasts as long as you want it to.

You are already whole and do not need healing. The illusion is the belief that you are not whole. You are already the improved version. You only hold illusions in the body.

If there is despair and darkness, pull up the blinds and let your inner light out. The darkness is there for contrast, to help you see the light inside you. You need only be who you are to release it. You belong to a race of heroes whose lineage goes back to the Light. Focus your attention on these affirmations: "I am victorious. I focus on the light."

There is Nothing Wrong with Mother Earth

Mother Earth is no wimp. Mother Earth knows that people come and people go, but she says, "I'll just wait patiently." It is egotistical to think that Earth can't take care of herself. After wars, when people are gone, Earth rejuvenates herself.

Program your planet for success by not believing her to be weak and shattered. The planet has amazing resiliency. When thinking about the environment and pollution, be positive and solution-oriented. Be in a position to clean things up by enhancing your own wealth.

Living with pollution is settling for just enough to get by, without wanting to make things better. A quality being wants a clean body and home. Pay attention to your own pollution in the form of thought negativity.

Thought affirms or negates life. There are only two paths. The negative thoughts we hold about Earth's condition create the cancer of Earth and murder the plants. Shower luminous, powerful thoughts toward Earth and you enliven her.

Earth has a gravitational center of negatively charged energy. This charge makes things heavy and keeps us from flying off the planet. Gravity is a necessary heavy force for Earth, but when it accumulates in a human, it destroys.

Masses of negativity in large cities attract other negative energies, and disasters happen. Earth pulls her negative energy back to the center where it belongs. Earth does not cooperate with people stealing negativity from her center. Tornadoes, volcanoes and earthquakes are Mother Earth saying, "Don't steal the heavy thoughts." People use heavy thoughts to tear things apart. Earth uses them to keep things together.

Sure, you and I and Earth have a few aches, but this life is all we've got. Recognize certain limitations and do your best.

Create a Great Movie of Life

What do you feel you deserve? Remember, God loves you completely and without judgment. What we believe we deserve, we get. If you believe you deserve punishment, pain, sickness or poverty, you get it. If you sincerely believe it is your Father's great pleasure to give you the Kingdom, comfort and joy are yours.

Renounce guilt, anger and envy. False religion's power lies in the fear that God will see you in your most embarrassing moments. However, God is all Light, and all Light does not see the darkness. Remember, Paul said, "I deem you not guilty" (Romans 8:30). There is no judgment, just cause and effect. You are loved unconditionally by the universe. Be who you are and see your own beauty. Lighten up and say "yes" to the banquet before you. Live it now.

The Secret Is There Is No Secret

Just do it. If you accept your responsibility to choose what you want, everything else will follow in its place. There is no secret. It simply is a matter of choice.

Go after what you want. When you see your ship coming in, swim out to meet it. Don't wait to get it from others. No one is going to rescue you from your decisions. Eventually, this reality squeezes out your best and brings you to your finest moment.

I (John Roberts) was a beginning solo pilot practicing stalls at 5,000 feet with 40 degrees of flaps, when my plane went into a dive and spin. I yelled, "God help me God" while my hands began moving in perfect precision, reaching out and manipulating first one control then another. Though I did not consciously know what I was doing, my hands acted with full knowledge. I leveled out at 400 feet above the Idaho desert.

Just do it, and you will discover that when you have done all you can, another power will help you. If you do all you can first, your spiritual connection will never fail you.

Chapter 8

Mastery

"The higher one climbs, the more rarefied the air,
and the more difficult each step becomes.
The peak is reserved for heroes alone."
—Peter Rosen

Drill Until You Hit What You Want

We may need to drill many dry holes before we develop the persistence to keep drilling until we hit water. Your early drillings take in the material aspects of your life: career, prosperity, relationships and health. These aspects take the largest drill bit. You have to solve the basics to concentrate on your spiritual work.

As you drill deeper, you narrow your focus and become more precise until your clarity has a needle-like penetration. As you go deeper within, your nervous system must resist tremendous pressure.

The pressure increases as your success grows, just as it does when a musician plays an instrument well enough to perform publicly. When you're very advanced and make a mistake, no one knows but you, yet you practice more because you want to bring out your best. This is the fine drill bit point of Itzhak Perlman when he plays the violin.

One day Mr. Royce was watching over a Rolls Royce factory from a balcony, and he heard an assembly line worker say, "That's good enough." Mr. Royce said, "Good enough? It's never good enough. That's why it's called a Rolls Royce." This attitude applies to our spiritual self, too.

As you keep drilling, your preparedness grows. With patience, you create a magnetic pull that draws to you what you've been preparing for. Remember, what you want wants you.

Mastery Starts Easily

Mastery begins easily and then gets a little harder. Like climbing a tall mountain, you start with a moderate grade that gets steeper as the views get better. You obtain mastery by never sacrificing your own integrity. You act from strength, not by going with the crowd.

Eagles don't flock together; they soar one at a time. Your heart will tell you how to soar. Your heart knows right from wrong. You strengthen your heart's guidance when you examine your beliefs. Otherwise, you dull your conscience with unexamined experience.

Make sure what you believe is true and it will influence your heart, freeing you to be strong. "When you are diamond-hearted, you know when, why and where you are going. The difference between glass and diamonds is obvious under pressure; glass cracks and falls apart, while diamonds maintain their luminous integrity."*

The diamond heart within you resists frustration. The process of dealing with your trials polishes you. Then, before you know it, you knock on the door of unalterable faith. You never tire of your persistence because you are strong. Tap, tap, tap and then boom! You've tapped your birthright — a dynamic, spiritual force-field.

Choose Your Beliefs Carefully

Spiritual development is simple, but it requires courage and drive. You need courage to take heart and examine your beliefs for truth. Your drive is your talent or innate ability.

Adolf Hitler said, "A lie repeated long enough is accepted as the truth." But if you listen in the silence, you know truth by how it resonates in your heart, soul and mind. If you look for facts your heart will not be overrun with lies. Choose your own way and believe only truth.

Nietzsche said, "There is my way and there is your way, but there is no *The Way*." Examine what is right for your way at this time. Which of your beliefs do you need to challenge and expose to the light of day? What new knowledge might benefit you?

Once, a monkey was trapped by reaching in a large earthen pot to grab a mango; it couldn't get its hand out with the mango in it. Rather than let go of the mango it stayed stuck and trapped. Beliefs can keep us stuck and trapped. Many beliefs promise a fruit they cannot deliver.

Disease results from a long period of unempowered thinking. Amazing healing can happen, but belief systems too often get in the way. Ask yourself how your beliefs affirm your life with light and love.

Karl Marx said, "Religion is the opium of the people." Religion and belief systems are often like life rafts. Float on your own instead of thrashing around. You don't need a life raft when you enjoy floating in the streams of life. Enjoy, relax and surrender to the flow of life, and enlightenment will be yours.

No Need to Evangelize

People who feel inadequate about the validity of their beliefs often evangelize so they can convince themselves. Do not criticize an opponent. It only shows your inadequacy. People spend most of their lives arguing over opinions rather than examining the foundation of their assumptions.

You only allow yourself to perceive certain things. In order to perceive something new, it must harmonize enough with what you already believe. Those in harmony with you understand you; those who are not, will not.

Mr. Sun and Mr. Wind were talking about how to get an older gentleman to take off his jacket as he sat on a park bench. Mr. Wind said, "I will just blow a little bit." As he blew, the man buttoned the coat up tighter. So he blew harder, and the man held on to his coat. Mr. Sun simply shined. His warm rays beamed down, and the man unbuttoned the coat. After a while, he took it off and laid it on the bench.

Shine your light and allow your warmth to radiate. Bless the earth by being pure, not by evangelizing.

Levels of Consciousness -- Energy Centers

Jacob "dreamed that he saw a stairway reaching from earth to heaven, with angels going up and coming down on it" (Genesis 28:12). This stairway, or the ladder rungs, have corollary energy centers in the body. Your thinking creates your nature, represented as a rung of the ladder.

Throughout the day you use different energy centers near various nerve plexuses. You develop your consciousness from the mundane to the transcendental. We can't stay high all the time, though this can be our primary operating level. The vibration of these centers changes throughout incarnations, and they gradually develop with the quality of your thought and emotion. The sign posts are all pointing up.

The first six levels of consciousness discussed below can all be worked on at the same time. Some of these concepts derive from teachings of Mystical Christianity.

First Rung -- Survival Energy Center

Physical location: Tail bone or perineum
Geographical location: Mouth of the Jordan River
Color: Red

This first center focuses on life-promoting energy, money and basic survival issues. You look at the world from this activity center, and its degree of development colors your view. Animals live on this level. Concerns with protection from violence or perpetrating violence originate in this center. Sexuality from this center is animalistic and impulsive, and most often concerned with reproduction. You must meet your basic survival needs before you can develop higher energy centers.

Second Rung -- Senses Center

Physical location:
  Genital organs, first lumbar vertebra, spleen
Geographical location: Bethany
Color: Orange

From the senses center you feel, taste, see, hear and develop exhilaration from your senses. From here you enjoy life, and become more sensual in your sexuality. You enjoy fine food, visual stimuli and music from this center. When you sense your physical world, things from all realms are at your disposal. Be aware of what you sense.

Third Rung -- Power Center
Physical location: Solar plexus, eighth thoracic vertebra
Geographical location: Jacob's Well
Color: Yellow

When this third center of power is highly charged, you have tremendous energy. You can stay up all night and feel refreshed. You can project your energy from this center to manifest in the world. You begin to qualify the plenty and explore the extent of your control. To develop this center, focus your energy on what you can influence. Feel from this center your power and energy. How much life force energy do you have? How far can you run? How long can you go without food or sleep?

The solar plexus is like a feeler. The solar plexus senses first, then thinks. The brain thinks, then feels. The gray matter of thinking is on the inside of the solar plexus, with the white matter of feeling on the outside. In the brain, it is just the opposite. The gray matter is on the outside and the white matter on the inside. Very sensitive to vibration, the solar plexus feels grating personalities quickly. When your belief system is threatened, it affects the solar plexus. If someone puts his hand or crosses his arms over his solar plexus, you or the subject of discussion probably threatens him.

A person's charisma emanates from the solar plexus. This huge bundle of electric energy can be like a big, radiant sun.

Fourth Rung -- Heart Center
Physical location: Heart plexus, first thoracic vertebra
Geographical location: Sea of Galilee
Color: Green

This fourth center exudes nurturing and conscious love. Can you love creepy crawly things or the meanest thing in the world and really feel the love? When you can do this, you have gotten to the heart center. You do not even hate when you are forced to defend yourself. First and foremost, you love yourself. Thinking and acting from the heart center, you love and are loved. Strong and powerful love heals your body. Love dissolves all darkness in your physical form. It keeps you youthful, powerful and alive as long as you choose.

Fifth Rung -- Creative Expression Center
Physical location: Third cervical (neck) vertebra
Geographical location: Lake Huleh
Color: Blue

When you have met your survival needs, controlled your senses, have power beyond fatigue and can love, you can create. When conscious from this fifth center, your heart overflows with love in the form of creative expression. You talk, write, paint, dance, design a workshop or build a house. Creative expression increases the flow of love coming through you, manifesting your talents to their fullest.

Sixth Rung -- Clairvoyant Center
Physical location:
  First cervical vertebra, pituitary and pineal glands
Geographical location: Road to Damascus
Color: Indigo

After you develop centers one through five enough to be responsible, love purifies the body. At the sixth center, you are not locked in by your belief systems, so you are open to new things. Your evaluations of the world are balanced. You can stop the thoughts, concentrate and meditate. You maintain your energy and stay centered. You see this glorious world in all its wonder. Your aura is so clear you can see beyond the realm of the usual world without bias.

Seventh Rung -- Heaven Center
Physical Location: Crown of head
Geographic Location: Mount Herman
Color: Pale purple

At this level we live in harmony and have laser-like focus. This center has to do with integration and transfiguration. It is the culmination of all the other energy centers and multiplies their power. The seventh center is a higher level of seeing. You've gone from the violet to the ultra-violet. Meditation gives birth to super-consciousness. From the ultraviolet, you finally burst into the white light and communicate on a higher plane. You enjoy a highly developed sense of commonwealth.

Attain Mastery

Sail your ship straight through the center, not as an extremist of either side. You get too close to a rocky shore by swinging to the extreme right or left. If you never see anything positive, you are shipwrecked by despair. If you are a Pollyanna who refuses to acknowledge negative energies, you're eaten by the sharks. Balanced energies are integrated in the center. When you get to the top rung, everything is integrated and you are centered.

To attain mastery, examine your life and beliefs by weighing the evidence truthfully. Honesty is a faculty of consciousness. Be scrupulously honest with your thoughts. You must be extremely conscious to see what the rational mind has concluded. This rational mind leads to your emotional state. Go back and determine if your conclusions were true or false. Your evaluations must be correct to maintain your balance. Watch the seasons of your emotions and see where they come from. When you're aware of how you think, you can know where your emotions begin. Peter says, "To master, control and understand the forces of mind and beyond is to hold destiny in your hands. This power can never be in the hands of those who would abuse it. The fail-safe system is virtue. Virtue comes to the surface in our lives after many, many years of refusing to whine or revile either ourselves or others. That means we have bathed ourselves in positive vibrations for a long time. For a long, long time we have not entertained a single negative expression."

Where Is the Cheese?

A psychology researcher put a rat in the central box of a maze with ten tunnels radiating from it. He put some cheese at the end of tunnel three and let the rat out. It wandered around and would on the third or fourth trial learn that the cheese was up tunnel three. Then, it would go there every time.

He then moved the cheese to tunnel seven. The rat continued going down tunnel three. But by the third or fourth trial, it would sniff around and soon find the cheese at the end of tunnel seven. Then he took all the cheese away. After three unsuccessful attempts the rat refused to go down the tunnels again.

The same sort of challenge faces us with our belief systems. Many of us still look down the same old tunnel for the cheese. We know that cheese used to be down tunnel three, and believe the cheese is supposed to be down tunnel three. Perhaps we were told it would always be down tunnel three. But there hasn't been any reward down that belief system tunnel in a long time.

We often want what we think should be, instead of facing the reality of what is. Sometimes we get trapped in belief tunnels that have no cheese at the end. We do this and then wonder why we are frustrated.

The rat changes tunnels because it wants the cheese. Are you going down any empty tunnels that no longer nourish you? Examine your beliefs for their practical rewards and discard those that don't nourish you. Beliefs don't erase facts. You can believe anything you want, but beliefs do not lead you to enlightenment.

The Frog in the Milk Pail

Put your will and imagination together, and you'll win what you desire. Sit quietly and write down all your thoughts for an hour. You will have a prophecy of your future in your hands. These thoughts become visualizations that create your reality.

You are the grand creator of your destiny on earth. Apply your visualization and your energy. What you think about you will get. We usually refuse to change until we see the train coming and then we say, "Oh, oh, maybe I shouldn't be parked on the tracks." Stop! Look! Listen! What dead end tunnels are you going down?

How energetically do you create what you want? Put your will and imagination together, then paddle your feet like the frog who fell in the milk pail. Rather than drown, it swam and swam until the milk turned to butter and it jumped out.

Change Addictions to Preferences

Don't become addicted to experiences, or your bubbles will burst. If a preference doesn't happen, so what? It was just a preference. Don't demand things. This allows you to live effortlessly. Renounce desire for enlightenment. When Jesus went into the wilderness, he dropped everything he had accumulated and went searching for truth.

When you empty yourself of your preconceived ideas, you go into the wilderness of your own being.

Jesus had 40 days of waiting with spiritual and physical hunger. Keep moving along the path through the scenery. You can't be filled with light when your cup overflows with belief. Empty yourself so you may fill with truth.

Situations change when you least expect it, but if you're a child of the Light no darkness can overtake you. "The Day of the Lord will come as a thief comes at night" (I Thessalonians 5:2). His coming is invisible, yet every eye of discernment, the developed third eye of clairvoyance, will see the Christ in all his glory.

He will return just as he promised. He was taken up by a cloud, no one else saw him, and he said he would reappear in a very similar way, invisibly, without notice or fanfare of trumpets blowing. He said he would be present (a presence) at the time of the end when many would benefit from this luminous presence. Only through spiritual discernment can we see the Christ energy. We discover its presence within us.

How Fully Do You Live?

Focus on living in perfect peace now. If you could live in perfect peace for the next six months and then die, how would you live those days? How would they differ from how you live now? Live that way today.

If you are not living vibrantly, you fear death because you don't live fully. Do not blame others for your circumstances or speak of limitations. Live life to the fullest.

What do you want to do now? If you do not say "yes" to happiness now, you get in a habit of postponing happiness. When did you plan on getting around to it? Happiness comes when you quit trying to find it. Happiness is your natural state. Happiness is only a decision away. Decide to be happy now.

Live the Vibrant Life Now

It can never be any time but now. Now is all you have. Are you okay right now? If not, what do you need to do differently? Do it. Be practical and begin now. Eternity is timeless. Living in the moment keeps you from worry. The word "worry" has its origin in the Celtic word "wrygen," which means to choke, strangle and suffocate. That is just what worry does.

The Samurai say, "Kings die, paupers die, but the Samurai know when and why." Once we accept our death, we live wholeheartedly.

Do not let the future take precedence over the present. It is today that you do the walking. You are rich indeed, because eternity is here and now. You can only age if you accelerate your future. Be meditatively present today.

Exciting events throw you immediately into the present. Someone parachuting is clearly in a meditative moment and fully conscious in the present. Can you remember an action time when you were fully in the present? Perhaps you were running bases, getting out of the path of an oncoming car or playing a stringed instrument. If so, you know meditation, the one-pointed mind focused on the present. Time seems suspended when we face danger, are concentrating or meditating.

Seize Your Day

The fullness of life is as temporary as a flower in bloom. The sunset is never the same. You can only see new ones and appreciate the moment. *Carpe diem* — seize the day. Live life now.

Enlightenment is often a sudden discovery of "I Am." The enlightened need not ask themselves, "What shall I play or work at today?" Life is a smorgasbord, a "taste it all" phenomenon and a precious flow of present experience.

We can only find the unseen Kingdom of Heaven in the seen. The unseen is within the seen. To experience life to the fullest, accept every experience as if it were the Kingdom of God. Then it is. Do not hold back out of fear of failure, embarrassment or belief in limitation.

Into the Moment

When Jesus spoke of the end of the world, it was a device to create a sense of urgency. All the great Masters have devices for creating a sense of urgency. They trick you into the moment.

Too often, devices lose their meaning and become rituals. The Bulgarian Master, Beinsa Douno, developed the paneurhythmy dance as a device, but it became a religion. The purpose, no matter what the tool, is to help you feel the moment of surprise when you realize something more. This moment of awe counts in your heart.

An Awakened Being

Only the awakened person functions successfully. The awakened person is aware. He doesn't stumble over rocks. He basically has no financial, domestic, emotional or physical problems. The awakened person creates challenges, but lives with humor as an ordinary being with extraordinary peace.

An awakened person has peace through it all. See yourself as a pillar, standing tall and firm even if those around you lose their peace. Acceptance decreases fear. The higher your level of awareness, the more you enjoy emotional freedom.

Acceptance Cuts All Else Away

We are restored to our rightful place when we understand our value and beauty. The music and colors of our energy resonate from us without speech. When we find life easy and accept it, our fear decreases, our auras dance with light and we rest assured that it is all perfect. If it is all perfect then even struggle becomes rest.

Our Thoughts Plant Poison Ivy or Zinnias

We can plant anything we choose. Our chosen thoughts plant the seeds and the universe brings circumstances that feed those seeds.

We insult the universe when we do not reveal the beautiful light bearers that we are. Light bearers multiply their gifts. They create zinnias, not poison ivy. They create beauty and abundance, not lack and limitation.

Develop your strengths and let go of limitations. The law of cause and effect insures that you don't get peaches from apple seeds, but that every time you plant peach seeds you get peaches.

If we plant the light seeds of Divine thoughts, we will know the luminous life. Christ was a luminous light form. He raised himself beyond human vision. Every unblinded eye sees the evidence of that presence. We can receive light and fill everything in our world with this light. We can create paradise.

Peter says, "When one powerful thought is held to the exclusion of all others, the longer it is held, the more electromagnetically charged it becomes until it bursts into light. Even one luminous thought held just but a short while will burn all dross from the gold of your being. When your concentration is laser-like the thought bursts into a literal, blinding light that you experience in your head. That is what I mean by luminous."

Everything you need for your growth is all around you, written in the invisible book of vibration. All of life offers opportunities to learn and develop, if you accept these opportunities. You start where you are, and then you are chosen for even greater work. Be spirited. Be aware. Choose what you plant and where. That way you will not be surprised by what grows in your garden.

Use Imagination and Will Together

Carefully visualize what you want. The circumstances in the outer world fit what you create on the inside. This works for creating anything, including addictions. Imagination always wins over will power, but using them together gives you mastery. Once you have mastery over yourself, the mastery expands to include other things. The reason you can't visualize enlightenment is because you can't see what you don't know. The energy can't radiate from you until it radiates in you.

Let the Sun Glow and Weave You in Its Light

We all seek mastery. The symbol of the cross unites the positive and negative. It also symbolically represents the number 4 of the Emperor in the tarot. The Emperor represents mastery. Legend has it that gold is solidified, condensed sunlight. When we become pure gold, we are golden-hearted and boundless. As the sun glows and our gold grows within, it is easy to drop dark thoughts. The sun magnetizes our light body step by step and draws us back to our source that is free of darkness.

Legend has it that the sun is bright because the entities who inhabit the sun have incredibly bright auras. The glory and magnitude of your possibility is incredible. The way home is clearer with each step you take. That is how weaving a light body works.

Attention nourishes the light body because attention focuses consciousness. We can fail any number of times, but living luminously makes it happen.

When you love the source of love that loves you, you sail straight through the pillars of Hercules, neither too far one way or another. Catch the feelings. They are more important than the words of the message. Come to know the luminous life. It will teach you how to shine like the sun.

F.E.A.R. — False Education Appearing Real

Dennis Waitley created this phrase to help us remember that our fears are based on falsehoods. Think about this for a moment. Look at whatever you fear and confront it. This is probably the most difficult thing you have to face. Learn everything you can about the thing you fear. You will probably find that it is something false you were told when you were young that was reinforced by others.

There is nothing in the universe to be afraid of. Until we overcome fear, it is an anchor that keeps us from moving. An enlightened being is without fear. Jesus said that if believers "pick up snakes or drink any poison, they will not be harmed" (Mark 16:18).

Whether it is true or not is irrelevant. It does make a beautiful point. The people in the early church believed an enlightened being like Christ could heal and work miracles. Jesus said, "Ye are gods" (John 10:34). He also said his students would do greater things than he did. When you believe you can do something, you usually find out you can. Educate yourself. If you have a fear of snakes, then learn about them. A child picks up the snake without fear until someone teaches him to be afraid.

The fear of tight places is the fear of not being able to move or function. A cave may indeed be a symbol of birth trauma, but nothing threatens a free man. A series of temples in India had openings in the shape of a womb that were narrow and difficult to pass through, symbolizing the need to drop extra baggage to enter the womb of rebirth.

You enter the "I Am-ness" by catching the light and the moment. One of the easiest times to do this is between waking and sleep. Too tired to resist, consciousness is there just enough to glimpse itself. Or, just before you sneeze, go within the pause. Catch the gong before it sounds and go with the pause. These moments can be of tremendous awareness. Light is found between the thoughts and ordinary consciousness.

When you see something for the first time and it is all new, you are free of judgments. The Kingdom is reserved for children who see everything as if seeing it freshly for the first time. It's like living in a constant flow of déjà vu. Everything is new, yet familiar. Look for God in every face, every action and in the pauses.

Innocence Allows Us to Walk on Water

There is a story of a Bishop who sailed to an island to visit three monks. He asked how they prayed, and they answered, "Thank you God for everything." The Bishop said, "What! You're not doing your other prayers?" He told them to do the proper prayers, not just "Thank you God."

The Bishop taught the monks additional prayers, but as the Bishop was leaving, the monks realized they had forgotten some of the words. They were afraid they wouldn't pray right, so they ran down to the shore. They saw the Bishop in his boat a short distance from the shore and ran across the water to ask him what they had forgotten.

That's the innocence of a child. That type of innocence surprises, empowers and frees you. With innocence you can walk on water. You become playful but not stupid. Innocent light-heartedness allows you into the Kingdom. To purify and perfect yourself, count your blessings and give thanks for your day.

Only the Strong Stay Around

Awareness is your safeguard. Look, watch and listen. The animals in the woods only strike or attack when they are afraid and cornered. Wolves eat the weak deer. Even chickens have their pecking order. This order operates spiritually, too. Entities in the invisible world feed on the spiritually weak and sick. Legend has it that many feeders stalk the spiritually weak.

Negative, complaining humans are picked on because negativity expresses weakness. Things we do in an unaware state cause us to be picked on. The universe exists for us to perfect our Being.

When we are our higher-level selves, we are seldom picked on. When a loving being is picked on, he gives a lesson of perfection. When Jesus was picked on, he never complained. Steadfast and serene, he spoke from his heart. Basically, Jesus said, "I forgive you for stabbing me. I know it's your role. Mine is to forgive you. This is what you came for. Do it." This is the essence of humility.

Act from the Inside Out

Jesus demonstrated awareness of purpose when he remembered it was his job to forgive, even when someone stabbed him. This awareness allows us to control our thoughts and emotions, a position of tremendous power.

Jesus taught, "Seek first the Kingdom, and all else will be given." Seek that indestructible essence within. Nothing can steal that inner peace. Hold on to that Eternal Principle, that mighty Spirit that gives you everything.

When the inside is right, everything on the outside changes. You become King of your world, in control of all thoughts, emotions and acts.

See Like an Eagle

An eagle can fly one mile up and still see a little mouse running through the brush. Eagles have incredibly accurate perception and get what they focus on.

If an eagle can see a Light Being they can see a light body. "The eagles gather where the body is" (Matthew 24:28). Eagles recognize an enlightened Being by seeing the light he emanates. To recognize the spirit, be sharp-sighted and decisive like the eagle and focused on the light.

Jesus taught that those who have eyes to see and ears to hear would sense truth in their hearts, and that knowing truth would set them free. Jesus displayed "agape," or "principled love." This type of love makes you fearless even of losing your life, because you know you live by high luminous standards. Empty yourself of all fears and negatives and fill with the Christ light and love.

Focus on Heroism, Not Fears

We don't slide into a gutter overnight. Our thinking takes us there step by step. Never give idle thoughts time to root. At first this is difficult, but before we can be initiated into the invisible world, we must purify our thoughts. This is why so few have been initiated into the invisible realm. But we can do it unless we believe we can't. Our beliefs either chain us in prison or open the gates of heaven.

Surround yourself with invisible helpers, luminous thoughts that become entities who do as you command. You are the master. Make your thoughts laser-sharp and precise. Your spirit guides will assist as you direct.

Refuse to entertain any thought detrimental to your well-being. What do you read at night before going to bed? What do you watch on television? If you go to sleep with your worries and fears you make it more difficult to get rid of them, because you have spent eight hours affirming what you want to banish from your life.

Cubing Energy

People either pollute or add energy to an area. In an Indian sweat ceremony, the energy cubes itself in the rock altar of the sweat lodge. Cubing means multiplication of an amount by the square of that amount — far beyond what seems reasonable.

There are healing areas where people go trusting that healing will occur, such as Lourdes in France, and healing does happen. The statues, rocks and soil have become impregnated with hopeful thoughts. They attract even more hopeful thoughts, producing a self-fulfilling prophecy of healing. This healing cubes itself and becomes even greater in those areas. Frequently, natural energy formations cube themselves on a mountain top.

Other areas become polluted by sticky thoughts. Idle thoughts attract harmful electrical energy fields. Some subway systems, like New York City's and Boston's, are this way. However, anytime your vibration level is high, lower vibrations will not adversely affect you. When you choose what you think, you have power and direction. You increase that power by slowing and focusing your thinking.

It Is a Good Day to Die

Life as you know it must end someday, at least for most of us. Live it with quality now.

Crow Indian wisdom includes this short statement: "It is a good day to die." This means to live vibrantly and enthusiastically, without regrets.

When you are enthused with the adventure of life, the exit will not be terrible, because you will not regret that you didn't live life to the fullest.

A Perfect Society

Honey bees are an example of a perfect society. They work together. Sensitive to color and smell, they dislike low vibrational dark colors. They see red as black. They will attack the color black, especially black velvet. Bees will leave you alone if you don't fear them. Bees love white or light colors. White makes them feel good and full of life. Legend has it that the goddess Venus gave the bees to earth to make honey. The earth got jealous and created the wasp that steals what others create.

To create a perfect society, we must watch, look and listen. The extraordinary person stops struggling and slows down to take the time to do what is necessary. Learn to discern who gives and who takes. Don't be like the lazy drone who gets thrown out of the hive in winter because he only took and didn't give. Be attuned to everything around you. Be aware of what is discordant. When you forget, become lazy or unaware, you get out of tune. Your world is as safe and prosperous as your thoughts.

Gain Speed, Lose Power

To gain mastery, you must go up a steep mystic mountain. If you try it in third gear, you'll never reach the top. Put yourself in first gear and go slowly, steadily and firmly. Find your footing and go forward inch by inch, step by step. Be content with steady progress. Keep your peace, keep plugging and enjoy the journey. Before you realize it, you are there.

Leave Footprints in the Sky

Many of us leave trudging footsteps in the sand. We make life too serious. Seriousness is the cancer of the soul. Leave your footprints in the sky.

Life involves challenge, but you can relax with the challenge. The day never comes when all of life is smooth. When you accept the mental and physical factors of challenges, they become effortless. Total acceptance of life isn't always easy, but you can refuse to suffer. Simply be aware when life is pleasant or when it is challenging and accept what is. Refuse to create drama around your difficulties.

Bliss comes when you respond to life in harmony and with choice. It is our birthright to have joy, to dance and laugh. Jesus spoke of being like little children. This includes being able to laugh. With people laughing, could we still have wars?

You Will Know Your Teacher

When the student is ready, his teacher will appear. You will know your teacher the way a salmon identifies the freshwater stream to follow home. Teachers are called by divine law to their position and role. "All things work together for good for them that love God, to them who are called according to his purpose. For whom he did foreknow, he also did predestinate to be conformed to the image of his Son, that he might be the firstborn among many whom he called, them he also justified: and whom he justified, them he also glorified" (Romans 8:28-30).

Always learn from one who is free and gives freedom. Look where the teacher is pointing. Is it toward freedom? A guru or teacher who does not give you freedom is not an awakened teacher. Never take advice from someone who hasn't done it. You don't go to a fat doctor if you want to be thin. If a teacher has truth, it glows in his face and he exhibits mental, physical and spiritual perfection. He has no financial or other problems. He has a twinkle in his eye and laughs with understanding. The charlatan doesn't know to be subtle. Look at people's hands, eyes and faces. Body language always tells the truth.

A false master points to himself as one with the answers, one who is better than you. Faith of any kind gives strength and gifts, so you can even learn from a false master. But with a real Master, something grows in your heart. You receive a superior element of spirit.

The Master's purpose is to free others, not to have disciples. Worshipping the aware person dishonors him. An awakened spiritual being, acting as a teacher, simply turns you back to yourself. A charlatan will never tell you that you don't need to return to him. A Master may. But a Master also may say, "Come back as friends."

Choose Authentic Masters

Jesus taught that the teacher will always be present in spirit form. Sometimes he is present in physical form as well. The real Master's value is at the nonverbal energy level. The Master's vibration creates a cellular vibration within you. Just as the moon pulls a great tide, your glands and blood are also pulled. The Master's tremendous magnetism constantly transmits messages and feelings.

The Master's subtle and contained spirit vibration is often the opposite of what you expect. Even if you don't see a Master a second time, the vibration grows subtly. You enjoy a different attitude and greater peace.

The lasting effect is like a farmer planting seeds in a very fertile field. The vibrations are the seeds of truth that touch your heart. You know when the seed has been placed inside you. You are the gardener and the crop.

A disciple learns from his experiences. We don't accidentally have brains. Sometimes we master an instinct and are honored for that accomplishment. There are higher and lower accomplishments.

Each person comes with a specific duty or call of his own. Some are attracted by Krishna, Jesus or Buddha. There are different nets and different baits. You will know when you are hooked. You have been hooked lifetimes before. A Master is willing to learn from every experience, too. The enlightened Master is very humble and needs no title. An authentic Master never gets offended.

Peace is not in the teaching. Peace is the energy beyond and behind the words. Feel what you feel. The silent teaching can't be taught, it can only be caught. The heart, not the head, digests the teaching.

An Awakened Person Is Happy and Laughs

An authentic Master laughs deeply and soulfully. Many unawakened people are serious, though solemnity can be a virtue. Some people love misery.

Peace, humor and laughter distinguish the light-hearted, awakened person. The awakened person has no heavy doctrine to teach. Giving up your negative ego means you have no more issues to defend. Being without defensiveness allows you to fully claim your authority.

Evangelism indicates insecurity about beliefs. Evangelists preach to prove their beliefs to themselves by convincing others they are true. Then they can say to themselves, "See, I convinced them, so they must be true."

Everyone has dramas. Certainly we can share with those who care to listen. Great spiritual teachers cannot hold back and not say anything. However, sharing is different from saying, "This is the way."

Claim Your Authority

Remember, Jesus said, "Ye are gods" (John 10:34). Why grovel when you can claim your authority?

You are what you worship. Make beauty your god. Strength, sensitivity, power, compassion, tenacity, peace and love are all beautiful. When you worship beauty, all you see and know becomes beauty. Hold high ideals. God is the highest and most beautiful ideal.

The source of your treasure has no end to its flow unless you turn the faucet off. You are a child of the

Kingdom. Claim your authority and your Kingdom, and your entire spiritual climate will change. Paradise is in your heart. You meet the eternal Master in the garden of your own godhood.

You are part of the harvest. In one of Jesus' parables, grapes represent the disciples close to the vine who are fed by its energy. When ripe, grapes soften, sweeten and fall into the wine press of God. The outer skin, the ego, is crushed as the best juices squeeze out into the vat to become the wine of God. As a disciple, you become that wine. Then you intoxicate others with the God spell.

Stop Blaming and Start Owning

Too many people blame others and themselves for weakness, lack of ability or laziness. In one version of the story of the Garden of Eden, Eve is tempted and tricked by her mind, represented by the serpent. She eats the forbidden fruit and then tempts Adam. She deceives Adam by blaming the snake and then Adam blames her. Thus the blame game begins.

Victim consciousness says, "Poor me, someone is always persecuting me." Our mind tempts us and we claim to be victims of something or someone outside ourselves. Many people fear the devil by thinking it's outside, not inside. For example, the TV evangelist Jimmy Swaggart implied that the devil forced him to get up at night, drive to a certain section of town and pick up prostitutes. Through his victim consciousness, he blamed the devil instead of taking responsibility for his choices. He so loudly condemned others' sins that the universe taught him a lesson in the blaming game. He must have forgotten Galatians 6:7, "A person will reap exactly what he plants."

For negative voodoo to work, one must have a victim consciousness. We can't be robbed unless we have a victim consciousness in the form of a fear of someone robbing us. If you know yourself, you walk with confidence, rather than exuding a victim consciousness. Criminals don't want a challenge, they want compliance. They don't want to fight. They want an easy mark.

The universe has a tendency to create what you believe. When you repeat a self-destructive pattern, you victimize yourself. Conscious confidence protects you from these fears.

The Original Sin

Legend has it that Adam and Eve were originally fed by God's light and the breath of life. They did not need carnal, solid food. God, seeing their desire for food, allowed them fruits and herbs, but they were not to eat the seeds of these. The eating of these seeds with their unique DNA formations would result in the emotions of guilt, fear and shame. Adam and Eve ate forbidden fruit of the Tree of the Knowledge of Good and Evil. Before this they had no understanding of right or wrong. Judgment started with the Tree of Knowledge of Good and Evil, and we lost our childlike innocence.

Adam and Eve were nude and beautiful. God, a great artist, had created them as beautiful, living sculptures, but Biblical translators judged it. Adam and Eve had been nude; the writers called them naked. Nudity is beautiful. Nakedness is harsh. For example, we talk about the sword being "a naked blade," not "a nude blade."

Some of the people who translated the Bible twisted things to manipulate the masses so that a few priests would hold the key to interpretation. Only select information was presented. For example, very few know that Judas was writing the War Scroll in the Scriptorium in Qumran at the same time some of the scriptures were recorded and translated there. Judas Iscariot succeeded Judas the Galilean, a zealot who wrote the War Scroll for political reasons. They planned to control the whole world by means of a 40-year war.

Similarly, the church was founded on control through guilt that results from judgment by others. This way the priests could control the many. Much of religion is based on the fear that God will expose us. This lie produces fear that feels real. If we believe it, fear can weave the fabric of our lives. Our fears keep us from our dignity.

Adam believed that he made a mistake, that his world was ruled by a vicious dictator and there was no unconditional love. He felt bad and ashamed. He felt guilt.

Too often you are taught to feel ashamed of yourself, rather than good. Your mistakes are just learning experiences, and the only true power ruling your world is love. "God is love" (I John 4:8). If you want God, immerse yourself in love. All teachers, knowledge, scripture and doctrine are sounding brass, unless you have love (I Corinthians 13:1). Live in the moment with the great white light of love.

Do Not Judge Others or Yourself

All things have balance. Even the hideous can bring us into balance, just as the atomic bomb motivates us to seek peace by threatening us with so much of what we don't want at the push of a button. Our own minds have all done terrible things. When we see the darker contrasts, we can fill ourselves with light instead of judging and falling into darkness. Adam and Eve came to feel shame once judgment occurred, so they hid in their garden. We hide too. We hide in shame.

Judging hurts others. We cannot hurt another person and be whole. Be happy around those you love, and that happiness will be healing. Sometimes we need to just zip our mouths. Smile and laugh a lot, even when loved ones do stupid things (which often are only things that *we* think are stupid).

Love more and demand less. Demand less fairness. Lots of anxieties come in life because we look for fairness. It is all just. We learn our lessons as they occur in life. Give less advice. Advice is taken only when the person really asks for answers. For example, when a smoker wants to see himself as a non-smoker and recognizes that he can become a non-smoker, he will be a non-smoker. Don't tell others what to do. Look how long it takes most of us to act on our own advice.

Let Your Light Shine

If you are embarrassed, you are either judging yourself or someone else. Adam and Eve were embarrassed, so they hid their nakedness. God reminded them, "I made you. I've seen you."

God says we are free and "not guilty" (Romans 8:33). But we say, "No, I am guilty. I am terrible." The purpose of Jesus is to remove the original sin of guilt that came into the world with Adam.

When we judge we are obsessed with what people think of us. It takes childlike innocence to be free from judging. Don't care so much about what people think. Be aware enough not to judge.

There is nothing wrong with us except the veil that keeps us from seeing who we are. Jesus says, "You are like light for the whole world. . . . No one lights a lamp and puts it under a basket; instead he puts it on the lampstand, where it gives light for everyone in the house" (Matthew 5:14-16). We weave those baskets of dark thoughts and judgements that cloud our auras and shade our light.

The Light Never Knows Darkness

The light chases darkness away. Think luminous thoughts. So what if you are dying? It's no big deal. You've done it before.

Life teaches you at a heart level beyond words. At this level you know you glow outside because you see your true self shining inside. If you see your own shining face, then make a toast to your universe and consciousness. You are the Light. Your life is a mirror. Everything reflects who you are.

Jesus

Jesus loved other people. Look at his personality. He was a good looking, single guy who celebrated life. He was very alive and practical. When Jesus told Mary Magdalene "Do not hold on to me" he was saying you can't possess me physically (John 20:17). But he told his disciples, "I will be with you always" (Matthew 28:20).

You don't have to have the body. You don't have to possess Jesus. Jesus' values were higher than physical, far beyond food and water. Jesus had self-respect and loved people. He wasn't public property and couldn't be owned, but his gifts could be invited. We can have the love that he is. Jesus is simply there in our hearts, inviting us to partake of his spirit, to be free and to love each other.

Sea of Galilee

When the disciples were crossing the sea of Galilee with Jesus, they had only been with the Teacher for a little while. They found the seas unpredictable and stormy. Jesus had fallen asleep in the bow of the boat when the storm came up.

Despite all the miracles Jesus had performed, the disciples were afraid they would drown. They woke the

Master and he rebuked them, saying, "What little faith you have" (Matthew 8:26). And he said, "Peace. Be still." The waves obeyed his will. There is a sleeping Christ within us.

Peace. Be Still

The sleeping Christ within will be strong when you need to use the force of the heavens. That sleeping Christ will command the winds and waves. Your life, the boat on the Sea of Galilee, will then travel a calm sea. The turbulent sea of your emotions and stormy air of your thoughts will come under your control. You can only be diverted momentarily from the path home. When you say to the storms, "Peace. Be still," they must obey.

When Jesus said, "Peace. Be still," he meant an absence of agitation or churning. Emotions are the sum of all our past conclusions, correct or incorrect. You set an emotion in motion by drawing conclusions. Once emotional, you have to ride out the emotional storm.

Don't judge yourself over emotions. Instead, draw the true conclusions that lead to healthy emotions. Then go back and listen to your self-talk and examine your conclusions to see how they led to that particular emotion.

In peace, there is no problem. Jesus was talking about awakening the peace from within. The heart interprets all things because the heart is driven by the spirit. Surrender to it. A new heaven and new earth occur when we recognize within ourselves the Christ force. Power under control is humility. Jesus taught that we grow by focusing our passion.

Focused passion is compassion, humility and power. "To have faith is to be sure of the things we hope for, to be certain of the things we cannot see" (Hebrews 11:1). "Sure" and "certain" mean facts. Build your faith on the hard rock foundation of facts that enable you to know without seeing and risk without hesitation.

You cannot be separated from this Christ energy. You can overcome anything. Your world is one of obstacles, and you grow as you overcome challenges. Take a few minutes to write down your challenges. How have you changed to meet them? You will change even more.

Courageous People Say "No" to Worry

Enter your deep recesses with the courage of a warrior to dispel your buried fears, those "what if" tapes that keep you from acting. Use the courage of your heart. You can change the negative energy of fear to the positive energy of courage.

We are heroic and victorious when we are courageous enough to say "No" to things we don't want.
Worry storms are thoughts that stir the winds of our
mind. When we send out worry vibrations, they
send electrical storms through our auric field and
the waves rise and fall. Suddenly, life is turbulent.
These winds start pushing the water of our emotions and we end up in choppy seas.

After the air stops moving, the water keeps churning. The waves roll inside our physical flesh for 48
hours after a worry storm. We set the dizzying physical storm in motion with one little thought. By the
time that storm subsides, we think another worry
and the choppy seas begin again.

Never discuss your problems with anyone who can't
help you solve them. Talking frequently about them
leads to more emotional storms, because the worry
thoughts grow with attention.

Life Is Our Responsibility

When we feel peace within, we experience the heav-
en realm. Discontentment and criticism comprise
the hell realm. The little devil of the ego on our
shoulder takes us back into the dead past and proves
to us our unworthiness to go on. This agent of darkness chains us to an ancient hell of memory.

Sure, you may have fallen down or failed, but it means nothing. Your only task and responsibility is to go forward. Let go of the old anchors of memory that have gotten you nowhere and live in this moment.

Imagine the coming months and years the way you want to live them. What do you want to do? Where do you want to be? With whom? Have you filled out your order form? Let the universe know clearly what you wish. If you don't choose, you get what's left. You are here to claim your birthright. When you act like a child of a King, the universe answers you affirmatively.

Your life can go one way or the other. You choose the direction. Choose calm sailing. Choose a beautiful peace. Let the clouds and darkness be behind you. Stay safe in the heart of the divine.

What a Mystery Lies in Love

The human spirit moves in us all, accomplishing and creating. Refuse limitation in your life, however it is thrown at you. Then you will know the tremendous mystery that lies in spirit and love. No one can know what your heart feels. How can you describe the intangible? The mystery is the joy.

This whole universe was a luminous thought that impregnated itself. We all have our roots in luminous thoughts that became gods and heroes. That core in us is the courage we explore and exemplify today. To be of the highest order, center and balance your life. Go straight through the middle, no matter what the challenge. We go to the extremes when we waver.

The balancing force is the miracle of love. Don't run to the extremes; love will lead the way. Over time, love will burn away the dross of impurities until there is nothing left to test. The light will come into you and radiate from you.

We have that magnetic force in us. When we become like pure gold, we require no more burning. We will be like the sun, able to do anything. Such is the miracle of love.

Chapter 9

Enlightenment

"Enlightenment refers to a light within.
There are two things present: one, light,
and two, the object that contains the light.
I call the light an abundant power
that allows life to take place.
What is the light placed in?
The self, the physical container.
I call the light 'honesty' for it will not allow
anything to be hidden from itself."
—Peter Rosen

Straight Through the Gates of Heaven

Only when you are comfortable can you hear enlightenment knock at your door. Once you get your momentum and direction up, you can go all the way through the gates of heaven. That is ecstasy.

Some people think wealth brings happiness, but where do you go if you have all that money can buy? Either you choose enlightenment or suicide. With poverty there is at least hope for wealth, but with wealth hope can die.

Once you discover enlightenment, you can never lose it. Racing toward it indicates insecurity and stupidity, like shooting an arrow at a target you cannot see and believing you'll hit it. The only path to follow to enlightenment is an aware surrender to living in the now. When you surrender, whether wealthy or poor, you are free. Seek only what cannot be destroyed.

Anticipate a positive future and savor a positive past. Above all, live in the moment. Bring out your best from your inner core, the center of your peaceful heart.

Only Buddha Knows the Buddha

You discern by first knowing who you are. Only a Buddha knows a Buddha. How do you discern authenticity? You discern others' authenticity by perceiving their physical nature. Your characteristics manifest physically in the way you walk and talk, as well as in your fragrance.

The issue is not "who is authentic," but whether or not "I am authentic." When we are free, we see everyone else's light. No one is higher or lower. Some have discovered freedom and power, some have not.

Reason gives birth to self-awareness. Self-awareness takes courage, even though awareness is as simple as walking across the floor and knowing you are walking across the floor. Facing yourself is spooky. It leads you to where the Heroes of Light face the ultimate.

Life is a love game, not a right or wrong game. You are unlimited. You can do anything you wish to do. Of course, you also reap what you sow. Do what you do, but be aware of the consequences. Destiny is not the goal, but the journey. Don't linger on the past or the future. You will be richer here in the moment.

Buddha said, "Come alone and without your ego" and meet me in the heart cave of rebirth. It takes great courage to come alone.

Multiple Personalities

We all may feel like we have multiple personalities at times. Find the ones you don't want, know you own the house they inhabit and throw them out.

We all have a crowd in our head of other people's opinions that we accept as truth. We're not free if we seek approval. If you feel possessed or controlled by anyone else and dwell on it, then you are. If you refuse to be, then you are not. Establish your truth and health and you'll be free.

Who Are You?

I am myself. Pray a time will come when you will never be sad or fearful. Pray a time will come when you wake up happy every morning. Pray a time will come when you are totally authentic.

Others accept or reject you for the image you create of yourself. So be authentic and let others accept or reject the real you. Who have you been? Who are you becoming? Who are you?

To see your infinite, perfect self, take a candle and put it off to the right side in front of a mirror. Turn the lights off. Look into your eyes without flinching or blinking and ask, "Who am I?" You will start to see all your changing faces. Your face may even disappear.

The day you disappear in the mirror, your original being looks from behind your eyes. You have lived a succession of incarnations, and you are none of them. They are but a flickering of life. You are far larger. You are infinite self.

Mistakes Are O.K.

When you believe you do not have power, you feel inadequate. When you feel inadequate, you are more likely to make mistakes.

Do not condemn your mistakes. Consider them your learning experiences. Do not take offense at them. When you take offense at your mistakes, you labor under such burdens of unworthiness that you feel life is out to get you. You feel victimized, and this often drives you crazy.

Perfection includes accepting your imperfection. Wouldn't it be wonderful if everyone you knew accepted you just as you are? You can start this by accepting your own imperfections. It is all right to make mistakes, as long as you stop making them. You learn new skills from your mistakes.

Peter says, "A swan can drink milk from the surface of a pond, and a special gland in the swan's mouth separates the milk from the water, enabling the swan to spit the water out. Take the best of this life, the cream of inner richness, and spit the world's water out." Keep what validates you, and let the rest go.

Feel the Unseen

A young girl with a box of crayons was drawing a picture. A man asked the little girl what she was drawing. She said, "A picture of God." The man said, "Do you know what God looks like?" The girl replied, "No, but I sure will when I'm finished."

Spirituality = Awareness

Spirituality means remaining aware. Remain aware that God is in the grand piano as much as in a beat up old guitar, in the flying bees as well as inside of you. The universe is impregnated with spirit. Heaven is on earth. That is what the Lord's Prayer is all about. If God is everywhere, where does judgment go? Judgment evaporates.

If God is everywhere, then God is in you. Your thinking determines your vision of who and where you are. Let awareness of God in everything empower your thoughts.

The light burns brightly when you know that today is a great day. Say, "Make another great day for me, Lord." Accepting our humanity is accepting our divinity. That is why so few people do it. Be divine. Your aliveness, your consciousness in the present moment, determines your life. Life is consciousness!

Courage to Love

We evolve spiritually by developing the courage to love, which rids us of fear. Recognize and accept that God is the one energy that fills all of us. Just be yourself. We don't have to prove that we are loving. Love is our energy. We show this through our respect and courage.

With nothing to defend and nothing to lose, we can be like the Master and exude peace. Silence speaks loudly. The glimmer of love in our eyes and the smiles on our faces tell others that there is something cooking in the kitchen.

Everything happens when the time is right. When we realize that there are no accidents, we can interpret situations with peace. Be determined to see things differently. No more malice. No more anger, resentfulness or fear. There is no danger when you are safely cradled in the arms of love.

When you are peaceful it shows in how you talk and walk. You simply say, "I am." Remind yourself to be relaxed, loving and kind today.

Walk in the Light

When you walk in the light you shine, and others see your light clearly. Your golden heart and luminous mind, not your emotions, will guide you. The

Kingdom of Light and Heart will walk you straight into happiness and joy.

Paul exhorts you to be blessed with wisdom and a revelation of accurate knowledge, and asks that you be opened to see God's light, "so that you will know what is the hope to which he has called you, how rich are the wonderful blessings he promises his people, and how very great is his power at work in us who believe" (Ephesians 1:18-19).

Setting Our Intention

Enlightenment gives birth to a new body and nervous system; a new golden bowl and silver cord. Jesus talked about his "light body." This light body is the resurrection into a new plane of living. Inside us is a light body that we can nurture to grow or neglect until it withers and dies. Some believe we must grow our own souls with the spirit God provides.

Tremendous responsibility comes with this realm of being. The moment we unleash the potential of growing into a light body, we must be consistently vigilant and responsible. We must stay awake to watch and listen. The secret of radiance is releasing addictions and being free to go and be whoever we want to be. God simply asks, "Are you free? Are you free of baggage?" The baggage is not your possessions, but your addictions. Your baggage owns you.

Nurture your light body with positive energy, or it will die before it develops fully. Much like the young oak sprouting from the acorn, this is our most dangerous period. Jesus said that once the salt has lost its saltiness it can't be restored. Being aware is the task. Watch, look, listen. What are you doing?

The Diamond Heart Is Within You

Great Sages inspire and hold onto the spirit of beauty in mankind. These Sages are a minority. They face great challenges, so they are chosen one by one for their work. People like Comte de Saint-Germain were chosen. Known as the mystery man of Europe, this 18th Century Count was held in high esteem by Louis XV. He influenced the French court and the entire continent. The Marquise de Pompadour claimed he had the secret of eternal youth. Comte de Saint-Germain said that the diamond heart does not break under pressure. Whatever happened, he remained so focused that his heart did not break. That is integrity!

"The difference between glass and diamonds is very obvious when they are under pressure: Glass cracks and falls apart, while diamonds prove to be the hardest, most durable material known to humankind. Yet they look alike to the untrained eye. How do you learn to see the difference? It's a matter of recognizing their brilliance and reflective quality. A diamond radiates light in a way that a piece of glass never can. What contributes to the development of this attribute? Perhaps it is the countless years of enduring the darkness and pressure experienced by a piece of carbon. I've often pondered: Could a diamond be in some way a drop of condensed sunlight? Whatever the case may be, I think we will all agree that diamonds are rare, luminous and valuable.

In this life you may be considered very fortunate to find these qualities in a person, and even more blessed to discover them within yourself. It is said we come from dust or clay and are animated by an unknown force. A diamond also comes from dust or clay but captivates us with its light. And while it is true that a piece of glass comes also from the same soil or clay, it lacks the light and force to move us.

The people who really move our hearts and minds are diamonds. They know their value and appreciate their inner richness. They are not cheap imitations or costume jewelry. They are the real thing, the rare gem in all its glory."*

Discriminate Between Kindness and Weakness

It is easy to be manipulated by "poor me" people. There are cases of genuine need, but people learn survival tactics. To avoid being used by someone, ask yourself if that person has self-respect and integrity. "If it is to be, it's up to me" applies to others, too.

Distinguishing between kindness and weakness takes careful thought, because often what appears kind is weak. Which are you being? Discerning the difference will save you a lot of heartache and aggravation. It takes personal integrity to apply this awareness. If you say "no" and someone tries to manipulate you through guilt, you know in your heart what is correct. You must stick to your decision. That gives you integrity. Heroes honor themselves and do not have a servitude attitude.

Make No Excuses for Being Your Best

We cripple ourselves when we try to dance to someone else's melody. Don't let a person or group of people distract you from your goal of being your best. Keep dancing to your own grand tune.

Albert Schweitzer said, "The greatest tragedy in this life is what dies within a man while he is still alive." Our spirit dies within us when we give away our hopes and dreams by agreeing with another's belief that we can't be what we are.

Say to yourself, "Yes, I can, I will, I Am." When you reach this place, you attain a higher rung on your ladder to heaven. You can break through in this lifetime.

Integrity develops just like a construction project. Developing integrity is a do-it-yourself project, an inside job. Practice first on easy things, then on harder ones.

Replenish Yourself

If you see beauty in yourself, you spend time receiving after giving. This is the time to fill your cup and increase the size of your vessel — your ceiling of consciousness, stable foundation and the breadth of your experience, awareness and emotions.

Are you choosing to give out and to receive? You cannot always have leisure, for without contrast you'll not appreciate it. Activity and time spent recharging are both essential for success in this life. When you have worked hard and created beauty in your life, rest and play provide wonderful contrast. Develop a quiet sanctuary where you receive beauty from the universe.

Examine Your Beliefs About the Soul

When does the soul enter the body, at conception or birth? Some people say that the soul enters at age four. Some say at different times with different circumstances. Some believe it never left you.

Some believe the clothing you choose to wear, the body, is also your choice. A soul choosing to incarnate may look around for certain genetic codes. Ruth Montgomery writes about this in *Strangers Among Us*.

Spirit Comes as a Helper

Love neutralizes karma and takes us directly to the light. Do not dwell on karma, or it becomes an excuse for not taking control of your life. Life is preordained only to the extent that you have free will and have chosen certain lessons and opportunities for growth.

What is God's will for you? It is your will. You must first know what you want. Your will becomes God's will. But you must surrender to the mission for which he calls you first. God gives us spirit which comes as a helper, not as your boss. God says, "I will pour out my Spirit on everyone" (Acts 2:17).

Know what you want. Spirit will help you if it is in harmony with your growth pattern. "Because those whom he gave his first recognition he also foreordained (or predestined) to be patterned in the image of his son. In that pattern is found the freedom of the sons of God and your will and God's will are one" (Romans 8:29).

Knowing of Your Death

You will know six months to two or three years before you leave your body. There is an ebb in the flow of your energy as it begins to move up and out.

Jesus knew of his ascension three and a half years before he died. A Master knows when he is ready to make the transition. The soul and psychic energy include unseen forces that in some individuals work in awesome and mysterious ways.

Enjoy the Journey

A young man was climbing a steep trail up Chimney Rock in the Great Smokies National Park. As soon as he reached the top he said, "This is beautiful," and was ready to go back down the trail. Don't rush towards heaven. Lots of us would get there and turn right around to come back.

Enjoy the journey. Each step is a goal in itself. Heaven is now. You might as well enjoy the process before you decide to start over again. Life is a process, not a destination. Many of us believe the paradigm of work hard, do good and get to heaven where you are surrounded by . . . what? Don't project your happiness away. God is right where you are.

The Story of the Old Lion

Once in a jungle an old and stately lion was lord of all he surveyed. One day the old lion looked out over the valley and noticed a herd of goats, which wasn't unusual, except in the middle of the goats there was a young lion. The old lion couldn't believe his eyes. The young lion was nibbling at the grass and making noise like a goat while scampering around and jumping on the rocks like the goats.

The puzzled old lion crept down the hill toward the valley to get a closer look. As he got closer his worst fears were confirmed. The young lion even smelled like a goat. The old lion decided then and there to do something about this young errant lion. He crept closer until he was right behind the lion and pounced on him.

Like a scared goat, the little lion squealed and fussed as it tried to escape, but the old lion dragged him by the nape of the neck up into the jungle to a still pond. He held the young lion's face just above the surface of the clear, smooth water and said, "Look. What do you see?" The young lion looked. He looked at his own reflection, then at the old lion next to him, and was puzzled by the resemblance.

Then the old lion took him up to his den, brought out a piece of meat, tossed it down in front of him and said, "Eat!" The young lion shook his head and said, "Oh no, I'm a vegetarian. I don't eat meat." The old lion came closer and again said, "Eat." The young lion backed against the wall, quivering.

The old lion said, "Well, you don't have to eat it right now but at least give it a sniff." The young lion felt something way down deep inside tell him it was okay to smell it. He crept closer and gave it a good whiff. "Um, not too bad," the young lion said. With the old lion's encouragement, the young lion licked the meat. He licked it again and again, then pounced on the meat, ripping it and voraciously swallowing it. Then he let out a roar heard throughout the valley. The young lion now knew he was not a goat, but a lion. It only took one old lion to show him the truth about who he was.

Like the confused lion cub, sometimes the old lion must drag us to the pond to look at ourselves. We have all nibbled at life. When we see we resemble the old lion, we can start tasting life. We will hear the roar of true self-knowledge echo through our awareness. The Master is always with us. We are not that far from the old lion.

Heroes Recognize Their Enlightenment

It requires perseverance to recognize who you are. We are uncut blocks, beautiful statues hidden in stone. This recognition takes a lot of chipping away by life.

When the universe works on us, some get the hammer and chisel and some get a polishing cloth. Life will always do what it takes to work away all that interferes with our beauty shining forth. Our beauty and richness are the natural qualities of a divine creature. We don't need anything outside ourselves, we only need to let some things go. Allow the Christ energy to chip away all the unwanted particles.

Life endlessly rolls like a river. There is no death; the river wears away our rough edges through our lives. The polishing and chiseling continues, so don't get addicted to this life. Remembering who we are releases us from fear so we can be enlightened heroes.

The Answer Is Inside You

There are no problems, only questions you don't know the answers to yet. To get the clear answer, be silent. You cannot live in constant chatter and hear the message. Spend some time quietly, patiently waiting and listening for the answers to your questions. Answers dissolve questions. The dissolution of the question proves the validity of the answer.

When you stop looking for outside crutches, you begin to sense the awesome mystery of your luminous life. Wear any costume you want — artist, homemaker, itinerant — it makes no difference. When the mental traffic stops, the lights go on.

Pause and be in the present. Desperation results from fearfully anticipating the future. If you are feeling desperate, come back to your center within.

Forget Your Crime Sheet

Life is magic when you can laugh and be childlike. Life at its highest value is spontaneous, in the "is-ness of the moment," without explanation.

People lose this spontaneity when they pile up mountains of memories, sit on top of them and add other stories to them. Holding on to one sad memory leads to other sad memories. Don't review old so-called evidence in your historical past to prove you're not worthy. Too many therapies focus on failure. Do not talk much about your past, even yesterday, because you end up living life through memories, rather than in the reality of the present.

Review your successes, not your failures. Forget your crime sheet. Forgive yourself by laughing at all your past mistakes. Memories that do not affirm life keep us from the good life.

The past and the future are both functions of the mind, but eternity is found at the center. The mind can only pause and stop at a place called the present. Practice the great art of centering. Life is magic when the present is the only moment.

Our Lessons Repeat Until We Learn Them

The enlightened person is the alchemist who changes problems into solutions. We repeat our lessons until we master them. We learn by accepting totally and unconditionally that life is perfect right now. Only then do we have freedom, for how can we change what we cannot accept?

When we believe there are no accidents, we do not judge ourselves when we are born with a club foot or develop cancer. We haven't learned our lessons yet. It's no big deal, just a fact. What causes illness? The root cause is thinking "I can't." Buddha said you are, this moment, the sum total of all your thoughts. "Suffering follows an evil thought as the wheels of a cart follow the oxen that draw it. Our life is shaped by our mind; we become what we think. Joy follows a pure thought like a shadow that never leaves" (*The Dhammapada* 1:1-2).

Ask yourself, "What have I learned today?" As we learn our lessons, life becomes easier and lighter. There comes a time when challenges still exist, but you no longer struggle with them. To live responsibly, be conscious and respond deliberately, rather than react unconsciously.

We find solutions and learn our lessons when our mind is not focused on the problem. Renounce problems. Just drop them. Only then can we choose the most beneficial solutions.

All a Divine Play

Solomon said, "There is nothing new under the sun" (Ecclesiastes 1:9). We are in a divine play we have been in before and will be in again. We all have opinions about how the play should be acted. We all have scripted roles to play and we do them perfectly. When the play ends and our costumes are off, no one can say who was king and who was slave. Do not get terribly concerned about petty things. Krishna saw that much of life is a great illusion.

One day, Krishna asks Narada Muni, "Please bring me a glass of water," so Narada crosses a dusty field and knocks on the door of a house. A beautiful maiden with big eyes like the moon comes to the door. Narada is captivated with what he sees, so one thing leads to another. She invites him into the house, they marry and have the prettiest and handsomest children anyone had ever seen. The sons and daughters grow up to be very wealthy, and Narada becomes the grand patriarch of a rich farmland valley filled with his relatives. Everyone prospers until a tremendous flood destroys everything in its path. It takes Narada's beautiful wife, his children and their children. Narada is suddenly left alone standing on a hilltop.

He hears someone giggling behind him. Narada turns around full of anger inspired by his tremendous grief. Krishna is there laughing, and says,

"Narada, where is my water?" Smiling, with a peacock feather in his hair, Krishna says, "It's all maya. It's all a divine play." Don't get caught in the web of maya, the great illusion.

Enlightened Humility

Think of enlightenment as a golden ripe wheat field. The green wheat stands straight and tall. The mature golden kernels bow their heads, humble with knowledge and discovery.

Jesus said, "He who is last shall be first and he who is first shall be last" (Matthew 19:30). Greatness is found in humility. Speak with authority and humility at the same time.

Remain Alive in the Now

We sleep too long. Unless we make decisions now, in this instant, we repeat the past over and over. We cannot choose life and let trivial issues bother us. Say "Now, this moment, I make a decision to change." Say "No" to the past. Say this often each day.

New decisions call for a new spirit. Expand and be strong and resilient enough to handle the expansions. Don't get distracted. Make bold decisions that choose life. Live your life dedicated to your greatest enlightenment. Never allow the darkness of the dead past to shade your light. Say "Yes" to the present.

Every seven years all cells in your body have replaced and renewed themselves. Old cells replicate old memories in new cells. That's how you age and get set in your ways. To release the influence and control of your past so you remain awake in the now, choose life in each moment. Fill each moment with a luminous reflection of peace.

It Is as It Is

Truth is simple. Living truth means living freedom. You can't have more freedom than you take responsibility for. Being responsible means being able to respond to life. Be spontaneous. If you want to laugh, laugh. If you want to cry, cry. Experience life simply as it is. Let your life be perfectly all right as it is right now.

Now You Are Free

Say "No" to worry. Replace worry with hopeful thoughts and thankfulness. Life consists of uncertainties. The word "life" has "if" in it because life is an iffy proposition. Allow life to flow without concern for every little issue.

Just before you fall asleep, there is a brief conscious space when you are neither awake nor asleep. From this "twilight zone" you can observe your dreams without being asleep. Just before this moment you can review the entire day's actions, thoughts and emotions backwards until you find yourself asleep that morning. This will improve your memory and allow you to recall all that you are thankful for that day.

Someday you may want to sit quietly in a favorite spot, perhaps by a lake, and just let the film roll backwards through the years and even lifetimes. Your memory will become laser-like. Your past becomes like an old re-run movie, and you realize the old tapes have no value. The movie is not the real you. Now you are free for life.

The Magic of Thanksgiving

When you go to sleep at night, count your blessings. Being thankful is one of the greatest gifts you can give to yourself. Write on a piece of paper all the day's blessings, and you will have sweet sleep. When you wake up in the morning, count your blessings.

When life gives us flowers, our thankfulness is the bouquet we give back. Be so joyful and peaceful that the world will never be the same. That is the magic of thanksgiving. It will change your life.

Each person has special gifts. Some may be more obvious than others, but we all have them. Which of your gifts does the person closest to you see? Which of your gifts does the world experience? Ask yourself, "For what virtues am I loved?" Improve your virtues and gifts.

If we are willing to dance through this joyous life, the flowers shower down on us. The Universe says, "Thank you for being the hero of Light that you are." A chorus of angels applauds and encourages us to shine so brightly that others may walk in our light with the greatest clarity.

And Then We Shall Know

A friend covers over the shortcomings of his brother or sister, minimizing flaws and maximizing virtues. What friends eat or worship makes no difference. In the words of Christ, "Love one another as I have loved you." Though no small endeavor, this small phrase is the key to the universe. Christ also said, "The greatest love a person can have for his friends is to give his life for them" (John 15:13).

The world is saved through love and love alone. If you have problems loving someone, love them more. Then you will shine like the sun. Love makes you friends with the universe. We are all here to be in harmony.

The love light is alive and glowing. Do not speak or evangelize. Does the sun advertise its light? Just love one another. Words are unnecessary. We are hearts, not just heads. What we feel is contagious.

Love each other. Then you shall know that Christ is here in brotherhood and friendship, one heart at a time.

May the fruit of your thoughts ripen
in the golden glow of God's love.
May we dance as the winds of God's
spirit gently embrace the golden field
of his harvest of hearts.

—Peter Rosen

A Visit to Peter's

The walk up the narrow, dirt road to Mystic Mountain, Peter and Ann's thirteen-acre estate, was refreshing the first time I traveled it one October day in 1991. Many trees still held their leaves, their colors bold and enlivening. From a vantage point on the road, I could see spectacular views of the Smoky Mountains of the Appalachian Range. I experienced a sense of pastoral bliss.

Peter and Ann's three-story, 24-room home is covered with hand split white oak shakes. As I approached, I saw three black bears on the road, relaxing near the steps to the door. The bears seemed to be content and enjoying themselves. I was quite startled by the scene and slightly hesitant as I passed within twenty feet of them.

After tentatively walking past the bears, Donna, a friend of Peter's who helps with the reception of attendees at the seminars and in making travel arrangements, met me at the door with a warm, welcoming hug and handed me a name tag. I removed my shoes, noting the custom, and helped myself to a pair of slipper socks kept in a large basket by the door.

I walked up the stairs to find a spacious room carpeted in thick, white plush, with white walls and a 17-foot cathedral ceiling parted with many skylights. A white grand piano sat before a two-story wall set with rows of door-sized double windows. These were framed with tree-like plants growing in huge pots. At one side, a stone fireplace climbed to the ceiling. Large logs snapped merrily, singing with life as they chased away the morning chill.

The seminar was to begin at 10 a.m. and close to a hundred of us sat quietly in anticipation of seeing Peter. Hal, a long-time friend of Peter's, played his guitar to begin our day, singing with his wife, Mindy, one of the songs inspired by Peter's teachings. Soon Peter appeared, his shoulder length golden hair and beard glinting in the morning light. His bright blue eyes met ours as he greeted us with a warm, loving smile. Ann, dressed in soft, light colored clothing that set off her long raven hair, went about the room inconspicuously, making people comfortable.

The way Peter stands, moves and talks always puts me at ease. He seems effortlessly balanced and indulges in no unconscious, nervous mannerisms. After meeting Peter, most people become more conscious of their posture. Peter usually wears light-colored clothing, and most people choose to dress in light pastels or whites, with occasionally some vibrant purples or enlivening greens. The colors red and black are all but absent, as are plaids and busy patterns. As a result, a calm energy soon pervades the room.

It is always a special experience to be on the mountain with its changing light and moods. Many birds, squirrels and bears are always present. Sometimes the sun dances through the leaves. Other times thunder rumbles while the wind rings the many wind chimes, often accentuating on cue a point Peter has made. I have been there when the electric power stayed on at the mountain even though it had gone off in the town below.

Peter's voice always resonates with kindness and assuredness. He never dictates or evangelizes. He simply shares what he has learned. He proves his knowledge by his beingness, his bearing and his obvious accomplishments. He can speak without notes for three days, drawing from his experiences, examined study and what he calls the "universal screen of consciousness." Peter expresses himself honestly. When he is compassionate, you feel his heart to be bigger than a lion's. When he feels like laughing, he roars, and when he is moved to cry, the tears flow gently, free of embarrassment.

Peter is both open and extremely private about his history. He tells of so many past occupations, places and events that he seems timeless. He doesn't talk about age or celebrate birthdays. If anyone lives forever, I'm betting on Peter. I've only seen him get younger in the years that I've known him. Throughout nineteen seminars, I have remained impressed by his poise, countenance and radiant health. He is just under six feet tall and strongly built.

One cannot help but notice his alertness and awareness. His treasure is a focused mind that does not harbor what-ifs, doubts and perceived limitations. He never tells you what to do or think, but stands as the example of what his teachings encompass. He challenges me to examine my thoughts and beliefs.

The clicks and whirs and badly-timed interruptions of tape recorders are not allowed to break the flow of attention and information. Many, like myself, take notes, trying to keep pace so we may savor every lesson in the future. Peter's exchanges with those of us attending are always warm and cordial. Frequently I see in his eyes the immense love he holds for us all. Many of us who receive his loving attention are humbled by his sharing. I have noticed that whenever he is close by, I catch a sweet, refreshing scent.

Peter believes in freedom. He doesn't meddle in others' business and does not allow others to meddle in his. His book *The Luminous Life* shows his name to be Peter Rosen, but he is addressed by all as "Peter." He doesn't advertise his seminars. If you ever happen to hear of them, he asks you to write and tell him why you would like to attend. Then he may send you a nontransferable invitation.

About the Cover

The most minor events can become highly unusual when dealing with Peter. Planning the cover of this book was no exception. I had thought of an idea for the artwork and had started the design process when Peter surprised me by calling from Tennessee one evening with a request. "John, I would like you to use a photo of golden wheat for the cover. I believe you can find the photograph of the scene I envisioned if you go to McCall. If you go straight down the main street of town, there's a little shop that is probably on the left side. When you enter the shop, go into a back room and look around. You may have to make a few more left turns before you find it. You'll find out."

Peter has never been to McCall, Idaho, though he was providing me with detailed directions easy enough for someone familiar with the area to follow with no difficulty! If it had been anyone else, I would have bombarded him with "How do you know?" questions, but I have learned enough about Peter over the last few years just to accept the miracles with as much grace and aplomb as I can muster . . . at least while I'm on the phone.

A few weeks later Chris and I were heading for the mountain resort town of McCall in search of the photo. Fifteen minutes before leaving, the phone rang. It was Peter: "By the way, John, the photo has the sun shining behind the full heads of wheat, making them glisten, and the sun is positioned directly in the center of the page." I responded, "Thank you, Peter, and it's on the left hand side of the road?" Peter assured me it was.

Chris and I worked our way up the left side of the main street of McCall, stopping at antique and gift stores and galleries. A young woman was just unlocking the shop door when we entered our fourth establishment. I told her what we were looking for, and she said she had a photograph just like it. It had been taken by Andy Burnett, but, Jodi, his wife, had picked it up just a few days earlier. She wrote down the Burnett phone number, and then offered to call them for us. Jodi answered and they immediately invited us out to their home and gave us directions.

We drove south on the highway, turned left, turned right into a subdivision, then we turned left on a small road, and then left again into their lane. *"A few more left turns," Peter had said.* True so far!

The Burnett's large white home has a gorgeous view of the surrounding mountains and valley. Andy and Jodi answered the door together and invited us into a spacious, light-filled home. Huge windows overlooked a waterfall they had created in their front yard. The carpeting was white, and we noticed they were wearing white socks. We took our shoes off, too, leaving them at the door, a custom Peter and Ann follow in their home on Mystic Mountain in Tennessee, and one that we have adopted.

They led us into a side room where Jodi had placed on an easel the large, framed photograph we sought. Andy said he had taken the photo of "the only wheat field I found, just north of McCall." He had titled it "Golden Wheat," and it portrayed what Peter had described so well to me over the phone: the sun, directly in the center of the page, shining from behind rich, ripe heads of wheat that slightly bowed as they glistened.

Peter, who many fondly call the "Magic Man," had once again worked his magic for us, as I am certain he will for you, if ever you get to meet him.

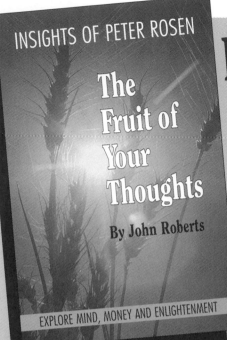

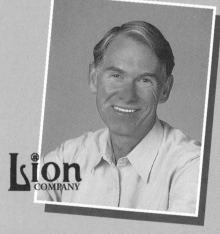